PURPOSE
BUILT
YOUNG

A Guide to Pioneering Your Journey · David Iskander

Connect

Book Website
purposebuiltyoung.com

Facebook
facebook.com/purposebuiltyoung/

Instagram
instagram.com/diskander/

YouTube
youtube.com/c/DavidIskander1

Copyright Information

Library of Congress Control Number: 2016958315
Pioneer Square, Los Alamitos, CALIFORNIA

ISBN-10:0-9978448-8-4
ISBN-13:978-0-9978448-8-7

Cover Design and Interior Design:
Gabe Ferreira (http://gabeferreira.com)

Editor:
Louise Bierig(http://www.the-efa.org/dir/memberinfo.php?mid=17523)

First Edition Fall 2016

Purpose Built Young:
A Guide to Pioneering Your Journey

Publisher:
Pioneer Square, LLC

For bulk purchases, mailing address, or speaking services, please email yourfriends@pioneersquare.co

Printed in United States.

10 9 8 7 6 5 4 3 2 1

He must behave like those archers who, if they are skillful, when the target seems too distant, know the capabilities of their bow and aim a good deal higher than their objective, not in order to shoot so high but so that by aiming high they can reach the target.

Niccolò Machiavelli
Author of The Prince (1532)

And God is able to make all grace abound to you, so that having all sufficiency in all things at all times, you may abound in every good work.

Second Epistle to the Corinthians

Acknowledgements

**With loads of amazing people to thank,
here are a select few:**

Jesus. Mom. Dad. My family. Nathan and Bec Bean.
Byron and Jeannette Culbertson. DeEdwin Washington.
Kenric Tran. Rose Han. Joel and Marie Holm.
Michael and Stephanie Moore. David and Erin Moore.
Sam and Awill Boyce. Joey and Rue Beason.
Cris and Melinda Tenorio.
Mike and Melvianne Andersen.

Cottonwood Church, Los Alamitos:
Pastor Bayless, Janet Conley, and the entire pastoral team.

Acknowledgements

Special thanks to my writing team:

Edwin Lai: This book would not be here today without you. When I wanted to quit, give up, and doubted, you kept me going. Thank you.

Gabe Ferreira: Your design for this book is superb. gabeferreira.com

Cale and Natalia Crawford: Thank you for everything. Your dedication to bringing this book to life is amazing.

typeninecreatives.com

Louise Bierig: You read through a whole lot of stuff to bring out the gold. Thank you.

Caleb Beason: Thank you for all your insight.

Michael Redding: You challenged me to always be better. Thank you.

Stacy Phung: For believing in me no matter what.

To my virtual mentors:

Author Launch AuthorLaunch.com
Seth Godin SethGodin.com
Dale Partridge StartUpCamp.com

Plus, all the books I read during the process of unearthing my purpose. PurposeBuiltYoung.com/resources

Table of Contents

Introduction

Part I: Your Story

Purpose

Part II: Your Character

Humility

Faith

Table of Contents

Preface

"I don't have a purpose,"
I said to myself, sitting with a pounding heart and aching head after a long day working for The Man.

More times than not, I feel I don't have a purpose.

I mean I know I have purpose, biblically speaking. Yet, when I show up to the classroom, the cubicle, even the church auditorium I have gotten this irritable feeling that comes back again and again.

I feel like I am on the wrong course. Like what I am doing and what I ought to be doing are two different things. Not all the time, but there are enough occurrences.

You probably have those moments, too. And if you have a crazy ambition, a high-calling, and an achiever mentality, but don't know what to do next, you find yourself reading this book. The way things are now are not enough.

You can't settle. You won't conform. Because settling and conforming, well, that in itself, is death.

You may be a college student, earning thousands of dollars of debt and still not know what you want to do with your life. It seems so wasted. It seems so empty. I've been there.

You can be caught right now driving to work, on your lunch break, or even in the middle of your cubicle reading this because something needs to change. And it needs to change fast.

The world tells us suck it up, enjoy weekends (I call them workends), and work hard/play hard as lifestyle goals. Yet, somewhere in-between it all, we find ourselves dumbfounded at how to live our lives with purpose, direction, and cause.

Your journey begins at the point of conflict.

When no one comes to give you a ride to your dream future, you must question everything you do (twice, with no assurance or guarantee) to try and find a successful, happy ending. Not success in the material sense, but the success that you were made for, that is, to be you.

I'm Not Blind

For most young adults, our parents had the option of a simpler, narrow path. Get an education (as education offered the path to 80 percent of stable careers), begin your career, and buy a home. Do a good job, get a few bonuses here and there, a promotion or two, and you are an A-class citizen.

Once upon a time, the American dream was coming to life for more and more Americans. People were gaining a livelihood they truly enjoyed. The middle class was on the rise. This was a relatively newer class system developed in the last 300 years. In general, America was serving better livelihoods for more people.

After the fall of America's great money system in the early twentieth century, pensions were developed. This was one of the first forms of security for the retiree. We used to have to work until we died (or someone could afford to care for us). The pension made us more self-sufficient and more sure of retirement. Add Social Security to that equation, and life was looking grand. Not to mention the start of the 401K. This let any common person invest in the stock market with less upfront capital. This meant that an average individual had more access to create the future they desired. The future was bright. In general, people were being given ways to have clearer direction for their lives.

Strictly speaking, life was simpler.

Each season discernibly held its own challenges and obstacles, but the formula went like this: get a college education, work your butt off for forty years and, ta-da, you were a provider for your family. Not only that, but you could also plan to relax at the end of your life because you had a pension, social security, and a 401k.

A happy ending, indeed.

Unfortunately, the story doesn't end there. The foundations we have been taught to depend on, the foundation our parents trusted, no longer provide any assurance.

Fast forward to the current era:

America is $19 trillion in debt (yes, trillion with a t).

Americans are $12 trillion in debt.

The average college graduate in 2016 walked out with $37K of debt.[1]

Plus, the average starting salary for those same grads is about $50K.[1] Which, could seem like a lot, but with college loans, a mortgage, a car payment, and everything else that life demands, a $100K salary can barely do the job. Once it was possible in the 1950s to achieve the American dream with a yearly salary less than $40K. Now, a $100k salary can barely maintain the cost of living for many people.

Why does this matter? Money has the power to form and shape our thinking and actions in ways that are unhealthy and incongruent to living out our purpose. Debt will keep people from pursuing their purpose and passions. And I have a firm belief that my time is too important just to fill it making money.

To my mom and dad, "I'm not blind." To our parents, "We're not blind." To America, with trillions of dollars of debt, "We are not blind!"

Most people die at 25 and aren't buried until 75.
BENJAMIN FRANKLIN, INVENTOR

Plus, we see education systems broken. It costs twenty years of monthly payments to get a four-year education (that takes five to six years to complete) and seldom does it guarantee a job. For the benefit of the doubt, it may secure you work. But, it cannot guarantee a job you enjoy. Education is no longer a key to a career, but only a tool.

Career lifespans are ranging into shorter and shorter terms. More and more people are being hired for projects rather than employment. When our parents would have one, maybe two jobs in their lifetime career, it looks like we will have somewhere in the range of twelve to fourteen jobs[2]. Not to mention we will probably get laid off from one, for no fault of our own. (Thank you to my first employer for letting me get that out of the way, early.)

We see pensions have failed, social security will be bankrupt by the time most of us are eligible to receive the benefits, and 401K plans went down the drain in the 2008 recession.

I don't know everything, but I can point out a broken system when I see one.

Everything our parents depended on, failed. It not only failed.

It failed miserably!

Our parents' foundation to life and happiness can no longer be ours.

Those in corporate circles today, who have the proper house (that is nearly paid off) and the nice retirement plan (401k and all) are quickly approaching their graduation from the corporate system into retirement. Many tend to live a dry, mundane day-to-day existence. They are walking corpses.

Does it make sense to spend the best years of your life waiting to live a dream (only to be old and grey and tired and needy) when you could discover

Purpose Built Young

your purpose today? No way, man!

This book is founded on similar, basic questions like:

If I have a purpose, what can I do now to actualize it? Will I allow someone else (a person in authority like a boss or parent) determine my relationship with God if I feel called, lead, or directed toward something they disapprove of? Can I prioritize a paycheck while living with God through every season? What does success look like when it is not centered on the self?

A lot of what our parents looked to, it's nothing we want. It's nothing I want. It's nothing us millennials hold dear.

And for the record's sake—please don't call us millennials. It's stereotypical and puts a lot of bad connotations on a people who seek fulfillment. It's wrong.

But, actually, since we are millennials, we don't mind what you call us.

Quarter-Life Crisis

I had no idea anyone called it a quarter-life crisis outside of myself. After I graduated college, I thought that my pain and suffering was my own sorrow for an over-ambitious youngster with no experience. I thought it was something I had to deal with alone.

Come to find out, a quarter-life crisis is a real thing. Before we can understand a quarter-life crisis, let's define midlife crisis. A midlife crisis usually comes after the age of forty. It happens because people feel the onset of old age ramping up. Their vision is worsening. Their hair is greyer. Their work isn't going in the direction that they had hoped it would when they were younger. A midlife crisis deals with a painful reality check often filled with regret and remorse from the past. Wealthy people experience it. People struggling to make due do too. It happens in the US as it happens in Asia or Europe.

A quarter life crisis has but little difference. It happens around the age of twenty. For me, it happened at twenty-four as I was graduating college. I remember how wonderful my graduation day was. It was filled with such good memories and people.

But the day before and the day after was hell. I had a deep sense of misstep as if, because I didn't know what was next, everything I had done to that point was a mistake.

Even though these are labeled as two different crises, I don't think they are. I think, for us millennials, this crisis happens earlier in life.

We are finding ourselves bombarded by the onslaught of opportunities mixed with the high hopes of making it big in a myriad of ways. This all leads to high levels of pressure on all our endeavors. We must be productive. We must be busy. We must be everything.

And, it reminds us how uncertainty for our future has increased. When you look at your future, you have (too) many options. Part of choosing one is renouncing all the others. You fear missing out on your purpose by following the wrong path. This feels like giant stones falling from the sky!

Yikes, and this is what we call normal life.

Purpose Built Young (PBY)

If a man knows not what harbor he seeks, any wind is the right wind.
LUCIUS ANNAEUS SENECA

You were made to be best in the world at something. Your highest return on this earth is to give the deepest level of impact, to your sphere of influence through love and service. And, be able to maintain yourself despite the ebbs and flow of commissary life (normal, everyday living).

In the hardest seasons of life, the most important thing to keep is the first thing we let go of. We compromise on our values. When it comes to it, what you do matters. And, in retrospect, what you do is a reflection of who you are. The pressure builds, and we topple under the weight of our world. When we disrespect, cuss, complain, gossip, stop showing up, stop reading our Bible, sleep in, spend money recklessly, eat junk food, we give up on our most important value in this world.

Purpose Built Young is for young adults to leverage the strong desire to overcome life's most crushing circumstances that keeps them from their dreams by detailing the most fundamental aspect of life—character.

Because God, and what the world asks of us is who you will become much more than what will you do.

The truth is that in every young adult I meet, nearly everyone struggles with little action on how to overcome the walls that blockade them from their goals. In turn, they have a passive belief system. Their hope has given up on their dreams. They sit and wait, watching Netflix, for the Lord to show up. When this happens their purpose is corrupted by fear. It's like taking cheap bribes.

Your heart's freedom is much more important than how people see you, what type of car you drive, and your accumulated wealth. That freedom is the way you will fulfill your purpose, achieve your goals, and live your dreams.

My Position

When I went looking for an answer to capture my strong desire to be all I was created to become, I couldn't find any solid material. I listened to sermons and read books but was given little clarity. And, I couldn't wait until I was fifty years old to understand. That would feel like an eternity.

With no solution in sight for my problem, I decided to do the study and create the solution. Socrates said, "When you want wisdom and insight as badly as you want to breathe, it is then you shall have it." With 700+ hours of working on bringing this idea to life, PBY was built for you to capitalize on your best potential.

The systems that are in place today for you to find purpose in your life are not enough. They have never been enough. They are scattered in church pews, verses, classrooms, and jobs. They have never been taken to one central location. Purpose Built Young is the organization of a wide range of teachings around the subject of Kingdom greatness and success; this book ties them together in a clear straightforward manner.

With that said, I am not a pastor or scholar or theologian. This book is much more about street knowledge, or simply put, practical knowledge. To live out God's promises in our life, we need strength, not only physically, but also emotionally. Emotional labor is necessary in today's world. It confronts the things that keep us from being generous, forgiving, and compassionate. And, there are no quick-fixes.

We have the tools that are necessary to make a world of change happen. We have to readjust our relationship to them.

Birth of PBY

For many, the best insight in this book will come from my current position in life.

As I write this manuscript, I am twenty-five years old. For a person to write on such a topic as purpose, it would make sense for that person to be a really old, wise person.

And of course their wisdom is extremely valuable. I gain wondrous insight from someone of aged wisdom and stature, an individual who is fifty steps ahead. But I also found another individual's advice to be life-giving.

The advice that really makes the most impact in my life is from the person who is two steps ahead of me. The ones who inspire us the most are the ones who can identify and articulate the fears and obstacles we are currently facing. Like a student learning new material, presenting it in a relevant way can make all the difference.

As C. S. Lewis put it, "It often happens that two schoolboys can solve difficulties in their work for one another better than the master can... The difficulty we want him to explain is one he has recently met. The expert met it so long ago that he has forgotten."

Think of your GPS that only tells you the next direction ahead (at most, two directions ahead). It does not tell you about the fourth, fifth, or sixth move forward. Because, in a lifelong journey, what is often most necessary to center your focus is what you will do next.

And oddly enough, the hardest step is usually the first step. When you want to go on a mission trip, the hardest part isn't raising the funds or flying for the first time. It is saying yes and committing.

I have a friend who decided to trek as a vagabond through different parts of the world. He is originally from South Africa and now he lives in Taiwan. When I spoke to him recently, he told me that the hardest part isn't finding a job in a new country or a place to live. Rather, it is buying the first plane ticket to leave.

When it comes to living with purpose, the hardest step is that you will need to shift your lifestyle from a reactionary existence to an intentional one. All it takes is your commitment, and that first yes can start the best journey of your life.

By and large, a person who is two steps ahead can bring out points of fear and championship much more vividly than someone who has not dealt with those fears for many years. They are closer to the frustration and difficulty that are currently pressing you. They can speak right to them. Address them. And help you overcome them.

If this is the hardest part—ust starting—it is the most important step you need to take. My goal in writing this book is to get you to your next step (maybe two).

Our Foundation

I have heard messages on purpose, read books on purpose, yet still was living a purposeless life. The first question I asked was, is this my fault? Is there something I did to deserve this? What do I lack? Come to find out, with a light study of scripture, I have a purpose. The question then became, how do I live it out?

I realized that God did not care as much about what I did as to the extent of the quality of person I was. "What he cares about," C. S. Lewis penned so well is, "that we should be creatures of a certain kind or quality—the kind of creatures He intended us to be—creatures related to Himself in a certain way." I was sick of waking up each day unsure of myself. My identity trying to be sorted every morning for the next 18 hours was too often, too soon, and too late. All that to say, I discovered that to find a sense of purpose in my life, it was not in the "successes" I built, but in the character I built. That my purpose begins to show itself as my quality is refined. Scripture is very clear about this. And because I won't be referencing scripture throughout the text (because the average person reading this already has a strong Biblical awareness), I included Appendix A for you to be assured the Biblical foundation of PBY.

When you decide to live on the foundation that purpose is unconditional and build your Suitcase Characteristics—humility, faith, and discipline, your life will naturally flow into its calling to pioneer. To see the framework of PBY, please go to Appendix B.

We will cover many different angles around living a life of purpose, character, and pioneering. It is essential that we discuss the key elements that surround these topic prior to diving into them.

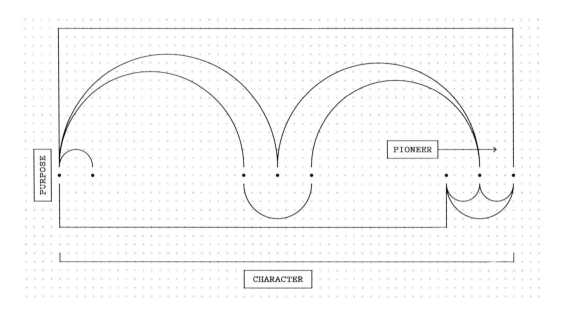

Visual 1: Natural Flow

Everyone has a purpose. Everyone. When you start from that foundation and build character, you gear your lifestyle toward unknown territory.
The only way to trek that unknown territory will be pioneering your journey.

Why Character?

What He [God] cares about is that we should be creatures of a certain kind or quality—the kind of creatures He intended us to be—creatures related to Himself in a certain way."

C. S. LEWIS, *MERE CHRISTIANITY*

Oysters create pearls. Pearls are rare, costly, and highly attractive. And pearls are formed in the oddest way. A pearl begins to form when a foreign object enters into the oyster body and cannot be expelled. That foreign object could be anything. For us, it is the fact that sin entered our lives. The snail must coat the foreign object because that foreign object could potentially threaten the entire life of the oyster.

The oyster than starts to create a coat, layer by layer, around this foreign object to defend itself. In the end, the pearl is created out of irritation, and you are given one of the world's most precious gems.

A seemingly tiny, insignificant snail creates a gem. How much more does your tiny, seemingly insignificant life have the potential to create? Could it be something even more beautiful?

A pearl is created by a common snail. It is not from a protégé, a score of wealth, or some undue power outside of the oyster. Every oyster can create a pearl. And, the oyster has everything it needs to create the gem, within. And yes, we all get a bit agitated by life. Something that is like a wrench in our spirit. A hardship we are called to withstand. A foreign substance slips in to destroy everything within us. We have a choice, just like an oyster, to create the most beautiful gem there is, that is stronger and more resilient that that foreign object.

In a pearl, the layers that build up the gem are called nacre. For us, we call it character. To be able to be a conduit for love and service, it begins with having a character that is submitted to building up layers of nacre.

Measurability

"If you can't measure it, you can't manage it."
PETER DRUCKER

Peter Drucker, a business management theorist that revolutionized corporate America, shaped management culture to put a high value on numbers. At the time, and for the purposes of his statement, he is accurate. It is worth your best effort to know what success looks like with a specific, measurable goal. Otherwise, how will you know when you succeed?

Today, knowledge workers tend towards busyness, a high number of meetings, and hours worked as a measure of progress. The challenge is that these things are rarely good measures of progress or achievement. For a knowledge base worker to demonstrate value in the absence of metrics, most people fall back on being busy and staying at the office later.

Undoubtedly, all of life doesn't work that way.

We have yet to find a practical and thorough way to measure character. Your moral intelligence is hard to put on a scale. And what millions have come to believe is simply what cannot be measured isn't worth achieving. It makes character seem less relevant.

In contrast, elementary school systems are beginning to make this shift. In May 2016, an article was written in The Atlantic. Paul Tough, author of Helping Children Succeed: What Works and Why, reestablishes the value of character in education. "Character matters. Researchers concerned with academic-achievement gaps have begun to study, with increasing interest and enthusiasm, a set of personal qualities-often referred to as non-cognitive skills, or character strengths-that include resilience, conscientiousness, optimism, self-control, and grit. These capacities generally aren't captured by our ubiquitous standardized tests, but they seem to make a big difference in the academic success of children.[1]"

Apparently, character is catching some wind.

Ironically, when we speak about character or the quality of an individual, we are referring to behaviors that are defined by a standard. The only way to have a standard is to be able to measure it. And that is to say, we may yet be able to specifically measure our character by a set of analytics, but we can still consider them carefully.

Researchers like Angela Duckworth, author or Grit and creator of the Grit Scale and founder of Character Lab, a nonprofit set out to advance the science and practice of character development, are finding ways to measure character. Though, many of the current practices are still imperfect. And, as David Brooks wrote in The Road to Character, "Most of us have clearer strategies for how to achieve career success than we do for how to develop a profound character."

What we are taught to measure are SAT scores, our academic honors, and our income. Yet, when school isn't your thing or when your passion leads you take a few jobs here and there that are not well paid, how do we provide opportunity for everyone to still achieve success? What if we are blocking people from reaching their full potential by limiting it to what is measurable? What if we are only making use of a small part of our physical and mental resources? Is there a way for everyone to be successful in life, regardless of their specific passion or how large their house is? How do we fill that gap?

What if, by developing who we are, we begin to fill the gap? We provide opportunities for everyone. What if, by measuring others by their character, we begin to utilize all the potential reserved in us? Then, we actually can know that we are successful. What makes a fast food job crummy isn't minimum wage or bad management. What makes a fast food job crummy is the person's character if their character is weak. Think about it. If you know that you have more potential in you, you will strive after it, despite your current circumstances. William James, in The Energies of Men, put it neatly, "The human individual lives usually far within his limits; he possesses powers of various sorts which he habitually fails to use. He energizes below his maximum, and he behaves below his optimum." Even if we cannot numerically measure our character (yet), we must develop our character. We mustn't become satisfied with being unsatisfied, and let all our extra potential wear away.

Maybe, just maybe, if we found value in building character, despite meticulous measuring methods, we would improve the quality of life for us and for those around us.

> In the Go! Guide's, you will find a resource to help you measure your character. Not by numbers, but by what we can test and improve by making benchmark goals for yourself. Marshall Goldsmith once said, "Everything is measurable if we're clever enough to see that it needs measuring."

The Vagabond in Action (Pack Light) The Suitcase Characteristics

We go to new destinations every day. We try new things, experience new moments, and live in constant transition. Our lives are being reinvented every moment. We are traveling.

Pick up your boarding pass and passport, head to the train, check-in to your hotel, check-out of the hostel, go across town, go across the station. Now try all these tasks while lugging around a fifty-pound suitcase.

In any good travel book, when it comes to packing a suitcase, there is one common and strong piece of advice: Pack light.

What you carry on the journey is important. The best advice is always to pack light, ultralight.

The Suitcase Characteristics assure that you have your daily essentials to succeed in life. Despite all the destinations and travels we will go through, there are key characteristics, we will call the Suitcase Characteristics, that you need wherever you go. The Suitcase Characteristics are humility, faith, and discipline. These characteristics are the Suitcase Characteristics, not because they are 'better' than other characteristics. Instead, by fostering these three characteristics, you carry what is foundational. Each characteristic has its own challengers. Challengers are what make each characteristic hard to follow.

Each Suitcase Characteristic has its challenger. That is, humilities challenger is suffering. When you face a circumstance of suffering, the first thing that will likely be challenged is your ability to keep a humble heart. Likewise, this is true with faith and its challenger doubt. Also, discipline and its challenger envy. When you see that these circumstances come to destroy your Suitcase Characteristics, you have a better aptitude to overcome them.

It's hard enough to carry or roll through a busy metropolitan underground public transportation system, not to mention going up and down large sets of stairs. Try standing in a busy metro system in Singapore, Berlin, or China with a bag that is twice your size. People start to look at you funny.

Each characteristic not only builds your ability, but is essential equipment for life's circumstances. It also compounds into other arenas of critical characteristics like grace, patience, self-control, persistence, resilience, grit, and tenacity.

Fire Your Digital Accountant

Today, you may make a mistake. You may sin. The way our system is wired, something oddly strange happens.

Your one, tiny, microscopic mistake, in the scope of your eternity, will attach itself to your digital accounting records. You have a digital account ledger, whether you know it or not. Your digital accountant automatically brings up the past. It could be ten years of struggle or a struggle from ten years ago. Your digital accountant is not helpful, but that's not his job. His job is to keep records and that's what he will do. When a tiny mistake draws ten years of pain, and God already forgave you for it, will you be paying the digital accountant for records you don't need to keep?

God isn't pulling up any records at any time against you. That's not how incorruptible love works. You shouldn't bring the past up either. This is the other side of trying to measure your character. You are stuck measuring how many times you sinned (or didn't sin), yet rarely find an adequate measure for how strong your character has developed.

Responding in guilt may develop short-term change. But, real change happens with an internal resolve. Why character? Because your internal resolve is what makes being humble, faithful, and disciplined so much more worth it.

Stop keeping accounting records you don't need.

Built from Fear

Character is not about the moral police coming by and commanding that you are wrong, wrong, wrong. You need to sleep early. You need to eat better. You need to sit straight. Don't do that! Don't go there!

Character is built through overcoming fear. Overcoming fear will curate the quality of person you want to become.

Want to be a leader? You must build the character to lead. And to build the character you must step into the fear of being inadequate. The fear of making a mistake.

Word: Imago (Latin: īmāgo)
Pronounced: i-ˈmä-gō
Definition (Latin): Image; a representation of a person or thing; Likeness; a reflection in a mirror.

Imago refers to the beauty of God's design in humankind. He designed us as a reflection of his image and likeness. When we say likeness, it refers to quality and character. Imago, where we get the modern word image, describes a reflection, of sorts. When imago first shows up in scripture (in Genesis), it's as if God is describing a selfie. At its first account, the human race was completely connected with God. Since then, we have become disconnected from God. Now, we are in a lifelong restoration process back to the imago of love, humility, and passion. When we build character, we are returning to the original image of God.

Want to be an entrepreneur? You will need the character to withstand the hard times. Step into the fear of failing. Step into the fear of not having a stable income.

Want to succeed at a long-term project? You need the character to preserve. To be resilient. To have tenacity. Then, step into the fear of missing out on events, gatherings, and such for staying focused. Step into the fear of being wrong. And the fear of regret. Character allows you to realize your value, despite the world's challenges. That is why character isn't an outward appearance.

But rather than just step softly into fear, Strong character means chasing the fears. It means stepping into that uncomfortable zone to build a new layer of nacre.

It could be the fear of losing your reputation... being judged. The fear of being inadequate. The fear that you won't succeed. The fear that you are unequipped. The fear that you will never be good enough. The fear that you will be found out.

The fear that you will make a mistake or fail. The fear that you will not win. The fear that someone will forever hold one single mistake against you, for the rest of your life.

The fear of looking fake. The fear of death. The fear of life. The fear of missing out. The fear that one day, you will look back and regret it. Everything.

Fear, in the broad-spectrum.

And, in the end, your ability to benefit the world is in direct proportion to the fears you overcome.

There is an African proverb that draws forth this point well. It reads, "When there is no enemy within, the enemies outside cannot hurt you."

The Hidden Gem

The scriptures are not clear (and with good reason) on how to identify person-specific calling. Our purpose, by nature, is deep.

Deep is the cry of unique, person-specific calling. On the other hand, scripture is unclouded when it comes to how to live.

Character is the game of ever-increasing irritation levels. If you are aware of your character, you will always be able to grow.

The same way pearls come from all around the world – Australia, China, Indonesia, Japan, Myanmar, South Africa, Scotland, the US, and Brazil, these common sand snails, become beautiful through the irritations of their life. When you say you don't want to go through a difficult set of circumstances, you are possibly trying to bypass an opportunity to become lovelier.

But when you understand this truth, you can ensure that every level of irritation can motivate you, build you, and bring out a quality in you that inspires and creates freedom and joy for others.

If your law had
not been my
delight, I would
have perished in
my affliction.

Psalms 119:92

Disclaimer

I invite you to suspend your disbelief of living a purposed life, if just for a moment.

I know this may seem skeptical but this book is worth every page and the few precious hours of your time that you invest in digesting the material. I ask you to devote to opening your perspective to a world known by many and only really being embraced by few. I invite you to begin to make your voice clear and confident—loud if it must and quiet if it wills, to the reality that your life was designed with a purpose. You may not see people living with purpose. Your definition of purposed living may be way different from your colleagues, friends, and fellow laymen. But, I invite you to open the doors of your heart and reengage with the topic afresh.

We live in the busiest time in history. Most people accomplish more in a day than one could do in a week just a few years ago. In that, this book will help you ease the burden by inspiring you to live the life you were destined to lead.

1

Your Story

Introduction

Life is potentially meaningful, under any circumstances, even those which are most miserable.

VIKTOR FRANKL, A HOLOCAUST SURVIVOR AND AUTHOR OF *MAN'S SEARCH FOR MEANING*

Skill, Competency, Knowledge, and Experience

In Luke's Gospel, the story launches right into twelve men who find themselves in a tight situation. Their leader, Jesus, was off doing crazy, unheard of stuff. He was setting off a movement. Imagine sitting and having lunch with Warren Buffet or Steve Jobs. Imagine how much people would pay to do this. Just picture sitting with someone you admire and sharing a table with them. Imagine how walking into the restaurant with them would feel.

So, as the disciples saw the miracles, when they were with Jesus and Jesus taught, they listened. They payed extra attention.

His disciples had eyewitness accounts of some of the best events in history. From healing the sick, to preaching with authority, to casting out demons, Jesus gave them one-of-a-kind experiences. Jesus was no joke. And the disciples knew it. So much so, that they gave up everything to follow him. Jesus awakened a deep desire in each of them to live a life bigger than themselves. This gave them energy. It gave them drive. It gave them enough reason to drop their current hopes, desires, and dreams to follow Him.

Then, Jesus instructs them: Let us get to the other side of that lake (the Sea of Galilee). The disciples—who were skilled sailors—listened and followed.

Mind you, it was not their first time on a boat. They grew up on boats. They saw their father's fish. They saw their father's work on vessels in all sorts of conditions. They too were well-equipped for the course across the lake. And, this was their hood. They knew the area well. At least, they were familiar with it.

Their skill, competency, knowledge, and experience equipped them for the task.

Well, we would have thought.

Fail

They all get into a boat. Jesus was there with them.

Jesus decides to take a nap. Visualize that for a moment. The disciples are in the perfect position.

After weeks of watching Jesus do Him, they had their chance to shine.

They were skilled sailors, who better to guide the ship!

This was their time to show off everything they had learned about staying calm, having peace, and trusting God.

They set off to cross the lake.

A little background on the lake: The lake is a harp-shaped body of water. This body of water was near the center of all of Jesus's ministry. He would use it as a reference point to his parables. This same body of water was the water he walked on. Just off the coast, he would also feed 5,000 people. Jesus performed ten of his thirty-three miracles right beside this particular lake[1].

While the disciples were crossing the lake, a storm began brewing.

In the Encyclopedia of the Bible, the author writes about the lake's position. This text gives us better insight into the natural condition of the waters.

The position of the lake in the Jordan rift is below sea level with the high mountains to the East and West creates a natural condition for storms. The cool air masses from the mountain heights rush down the steep slopes with great force causing violent eruptions of the lake. Such tempests are not infrequent and are extremely dangerous to small craft.

So, the professional, life-long sailors—who are well-educated around tides and vessels—were almost set up! This was their opportunity to make Jesus proud!

Get this, Jesus is asleep. Trained sailors get assigned the task to get him across the lake.

I picture the disciples chatting and saying, just think, when Jesus wakes up we can tell him, "Jesus, you would have never believed it, but we hit some pretty nasty waters out their last night. Now, we won't brag but, we put in work to keep you safe. But no worries, keeping you safe and making sure you slept sound the entire was our main goal. We got you Jesus!"

"Oh, and by the way, how was your nap?"

Jesus, fully rested, would be ready to do his thing on the next leg of the journey.

At any rate, in Luke 8, as the storm hit the disciples woke Jesus from his nap and this is how the disciples respond:

"Master, Master, we are PERISHING!"

Fail.

These were skilled sailors! They had every reason to conquer this storm. They had everything within their ability to team together, take on the storm, and get to the other side of the lake safely. They had Jesus on the boat, for crying out loud!

The disciples totally failed.

Or Did They?

In Mark's Gospel, the same story reads, "Jesus, *do you not care* that we are perishing" (emphasis added)?

The disciples went from seeing Jesus heal the sick, feed strangers, and cast out demons just days before. What changed?

I love the way the disciples responded. Well, not really. But, what you can see is that the disciples were missing something. What would cause the disciples to go from being mesmerized (enough to drop everything they owned) to thinking He doesn't care? What was missing?

Everything the disciples had experienced had yet to infiltrate their inner being. The disciples had experienced the power from the sidelines. Now, they were in the game. Jesus nails it on the head right away when he answers the disciple's plea.

He gets up.

Calms the storm.

And with all objectivity and peace, looks to his disciples and asks, "What are you afraid of?"

So, what are you Afraid of?

The disciples may have given up everything they had to follow Jesus, but they still lacked in one key area of life.

The Bible is scattered with examples of the power of God working from the inside out. This was a moment where the disciples had the strongest external understanding (skill guiding a boat, competency in the nuances of sailing across the lake, knowledge and experience in previous sailing experiences). Yet, with all the skill, competency, and knowledge they had PLUS being with Jesus while he healed the sick, released people from sin, and raised people from the dead, the disciples still did not have it within themselves.

They failed.

Or, at least, the moment revealed to them that they lacked internal strength.

When we talk about internal strength, let's refer to what gives someone the ability to withstand the storm of life. Internal strength (or internal sovereignty, both are used interchangeably) refers to one's ability to overcome their fears.

This internal quality, my friend, is built through the development of your character. And the development of your character is built through chasing your fears.

Fear: Part I

Let me assert my firm belief that the only thing we have to fear is fear itself—nameless, unreasoning, unjustified, terror which paralyzes needed efforts to convert retreat into advance.

FRANKLIN D. ROOSEVELT DURING HIS FIRST INAUGURAL ADDRESS IN 1933, AS THE GREAT DEPRESSION HAD REACHED AN ALL-TIME LOW

The biggest challenge is not necessarily a certain type of fear, though one fear may be very challenging to overcome. Rather, it is the lack of understanding of any certain fear.

Fear will make life feel as if the things that are truly worth fighting for are insignificant, untrue, and non-substantial. Often, when fear is drowning you out that is a good indicator of something else. Namely, there is something that is significant, very true, and important on the other side.

Once you understand a fear, you know how it operates and what triggers it in your life, you gain leverage to tackle it confidently.

Pilots learn to take on the winds of the sky, not by ignoring them, as if they didn't exist, but rather by learning about how wind works so that the pilots can adjust accordingly. The wind is spontaneous and uncontrollable. And this makes wind very powerful.

Just like a pilot learns how to adjust when the wind picks up, we must learn how to confront fear (not reject or ignore it).

Fear has much less authoritative power than wind. The wind can blow you away. Fear can only nudge and call and ask for more attention and recognition and try to influence your decision making.

Fear is always asking for a vote, despite what season it is. The more you know how to address the fear, the better you get at confronting the fear. And fear will be your biggest enemy toward living a life of purpose.

Universal Fear

Fear is universal. Everyone faces fear. Fear inhibits millions of people from doing what they know is right, and settling for less. Most people, who live in a civilized economy don't face the fear of life-threatening decisions. When someone fears confronting a repressive dictatorship, they may be putting their parents, wife, and children in the line of fire. For most the world, though, this is not the case. The only thing on the line is a bit of pride and reputation.

Unhealthy fear is simply any fear that inhibits you from actualizing your person-specific purpose. And this happens often. Too often. It's easier to live out your fears than it is to face them. And the universal truth about fear is that it begets more fear.

On the other hand, freedom begets freedom.

Fear is universal. But so is freedom.

Healthy Fear

It is easy to get the story of fear confused and jumbled.

Let's clear it up.

Fear is good until the point it hinders life (growth, building, improvement). Fear is good when it saves us from skating on glass-thin ice during winter. It is not fearlessness that is the end course for chasing your fears. Elizabeth Gilbert puts it this way, "The only truly fearless people I've ever met were straight-up sociopaths and a few exceptionally reckless three-year-olds..." Fear is important to us when it keeps us from jumping off a high ledge or trying to touch poisonous snakes. It helps us stay alive. Fear is good until it begins to creep into our purpose. Until it takes away from (living) life.

Healthy fear is the fear of God (and knowing that knifes are sharp and could hurt).

And the fear of God is to follow his instructions—that is the beginning of all knowledge and wisdom.

Your Greatest Strength

To take the first step forward, it is important to know: Your greatest strength is on the other side of your deepest fear.

For instance, people who want to be unequivocal in their ability to deliver the Word of God to unreached peoples will find a major fear that they must face is the fear of judgement. Their greatest strength is almost attached to their deepest fear.

Thus, your ability to walk in purpose will be when you confront your deepest fear.

Defending Fear

Interestingly enough, most people tend to defend their fear with excuses or insensible common sense. The traffic was worse than normal today. I don't have enough time. I don't have enough money. I don't have experience. Or, this is who I am. I can never do that.

It sounds a bit crazy, but this is the thing that holds people back from hitting the dance floor until their favorite track comes on. This is what keeps people from shipping their first project because it is not 'fully' ready.

We defend our fear because fear operates on the notes our comfort zone currently likes to play. Fear talks with bravado, never humility, grace, or peace. And it always, always uses excuses as its front.

So, What's Stopping You

It's not the world. It's not income. It's not resources. It's not the lack of people around you. It's not a lack of time. It's not your ex. It's not your parents' lack of love. It's not your boss. It's not social pressure. It's not setbacks (even though each of these can play a big role in your life).

It's fear.

Fear: Part II

Let's review the ten most common fears a young adult faces while pioneering their journey.

To note, each fear we discuss here has a corresponding lack. For instance, if somebody fears never being happy, they lack contentment. The lack is the key to unlocking unrealized value from within you. Further, the hero/heroine section will help you realize a concrete way to overcome each fear.

Fear will creep into your relationships, your business, your classroom, your future, your calling, your identity, your purpose, and your time. Because the biggest thing keeping you from your purpose is not a lack of money or time or a bad economy. It is fear.

> Be open and transparent with yourself. Don't assume too quickly that a fear is beneath you without first confronting it head on. There are fears that are so insidious and unknown to us that they cause us pain, and we don't even know about it.

1. The Fear of Making Mistakes

This fear causes you to only commit when the stakes are highly in favor of winning. A perfectionist in camouflage. The fear will say: don't do things you are uncertain on how to complete. This is what fixes people on starting new projects, but rarely finishing. This fear is dealing with an eroding pressure to always improve before doing. Preparation before commitment is often the fear of making a mistake in disguise.

Heroine: Courage

Can you try something new? Can you ship projects earlier than perfect? A way to test this is to do something or commit to a project that isn't a passion project. From there, make room to potentially make a mistake, and watch how people respond. It's not as bad as you imagined.

Niels Bohr said, "An expert is a man who has made all the mistakes which can be made, in a narrow field." Become an expert.

2. The Fear of Being Alone

You don't necessarily have to be alone to feel alone. You can be with 1,000 people and still feel isolated. Occasionally, this fear will masquerade with an agenda: get loads of attention. It could be positive or negative attention. The fear of being alone just doesn't want to be alone. At this time, you would rather be loud and noticed than quiet and at peace. The fear of being alone can look for love in all the wrong places; it can also be a source of unfriendliness. Sabotaging relationships is easy for this fear. Becoming a friend, being interested in other people's well-being, and listening is much harder. Many bad relationships begin in the fear of being alone.

Hero: Security

Can you find belonging, considering that, yes, you may be imperfect and face some major difficulties? Everyone is internally wired to depend on each other. There is nothing wrong with that. At the same time, spend three minutes a day by yourself. Set a timer, turn off or mute your devices, and all other noise. Be completely silent with yourself. Find security in who you are with and without people.

3. The Fear of Failure

This fear is widespread. Millions of amazing projects have been lost because of this fear. Procrastination on a project is just the fear of failure hiding. The belief that failing is worse than shipping a project is what causes this fear to win.

The fear of failure stops you from hitting the dance floor of life, trying new things, committing and shipping creative projects, and talking to strangers who seem interesting.

Heroine: Tenacity

Can you achieve your goal? If you knew you would succeed by seeing something to the end, no matter what, what would you set out to do? What chances would you take today?

Better yet, what can you do that you would get back up from failure (again and again) unfazed? Having tenacity gives you the ability to push through the noise of commissary life and see the value in every season.

4. The Fear of Regret

This fear will paralyze us from achieving your future goals. When this deeply internal fear plays on our past, it will take situations that didn't go according to 'plan,' and use them as evidence of why trying new things is not a good idea. The fear of regret uses our past to stop you from trying new things. Ironically, we end up regretting what we didn't do. Do you see how self-sabotage plays a large role here?

The fear of regret will warn you not to do something for the sake of "not looking stupid." I remember when I was at a meeting and heard someone say they wanted to try a new plan. Another individual across the room said, "Fine, but don't make me look stupid." It's hard to grow in life if we take this approach.

Finally, this fear will tell the listener: Whatever choice I make, I cannot regret. Therefore, choices are very passive or never actually made, which only leads to more regret.

Heroine: Grace

Everyone has done and will continue to do things they regret. The challenge is giving yourself the room to do so. Most of the time, they are not life threatening nor are they permanent (though, that's how the fear makes it look). Ask yourself what is important now?

When it comes to our future, learning to live with an openness to embrace uncertainty and change will certainly relieve this fear. When past regrets, self-pity, and shame arise, tell the story of grace again and again.

5. The Fear of Missing Out

This fear hates telling someone these two letters, N.O. Friends invite you out, you say yes, but you mean no. Somehow, a tail wind blew your head in the wrong direction. This one costs people much of their time and energy. They try to do everything and lose the ability to focus on what is important. This fear wants to say yes to everything.

Heroine: Purpose

If you are set out on earth with a purpose, can you say yes to everything? The obvious answer is no. No one ever fully utilized their resources for the Kingdom by being subject to another person's priorities.

6. The Fear of Happiness

This fear makes it feel like you don't deserve to enjoy life. It makes it feel as if you are lazy because if you are happy then you are not a hard worker. If you are happy, this fear will tell you something bad will happen. This fear will make a person avoid fun events so they can wallow in pity. This fear makes it hard to enjoy the pleasures God gives us struggling to trust positive feelings. It also makes even the slightest good seem irrelevant.

This fear impacts more people than I can imagine. When people complain about the good things in their life, they let go of their obligation to enjoy what they have been blessed with. This is the disguise of the fear of happiness. Think about it. If you complain about the good in your life, what are you covering up? Because happiness asks you to enjoy what you have and be content.

Hero: Contentment

Can you look around your life right now and begin to say thank you? Thank you for the simplest things like a blue sky, the feeling of the breeze on your skin, or the comfort of your bed? Your cup of coffee isn't a routine; it is a blessing. The fear of happiness looks at contentment as laziness or a lack of responsibility.

It's very easy to wrap our happiness in a distant future. Consider this regretful phrase, 'I will be happy when..."

Happiness is not dependent on some change in circumstance or having more money. It isn't dependent on the right job, finding Mr. or Mrs. Right, or buying a new car.

These things are not going to give you ultimate happiness. This simple lie will steal your life's work from you.

Whether you are in a hospital bed or a stormy season, your life's work cannot be wrapped up in the next season without smiling and knowing that this season is awesome, too.

7. The Fear of Success

This fear is the most misunderstood. The fear of success is primarily based in the idea that, if I succeed, will I be able to sustain my success? If I tell someone about Jesus and they say yes, will I be able to live everything I told them about?

Or, the fear may be if I do succeed, will I be able to top my success? Will it all end there? Will my 15-minutes of fame be over before I know it?

This leads to people feeling guilty that they are successful, driven, passionate, or devoted. This fear makes it feel as if you don't deserve more. It's counterintuitive to a content heart. A content heart is a heart that could enjoy today and strive for a better future.

Hero: Calling

When you sense your calling in your life's work, it is not so much about the outcome as it is about the adventure. You are successful and you will be successful. But that's not always the point. It is to answer the call life gives you. It's about rising to the occasion.

8. The Fear of Unproductivity

In modern society, this fear is disguised as virtuous. The hustle is great. I commend it. Busyness, for the sake of busyness, is a sign of estrangement to one's actual duty.

The fear of unproductivity comes when people find themselves with a little free time and resort to doing something rather than doing nothing. Because doing nothing is wasting time, and we have so many good things we ought to be doing.

This isn't based on the number of hours you work. It's based on your relationship to what you do. If you work for the sake of work, you have the fear of being unproductive.

We can easily quicken ourselves to a life of constant busyness. Always rushing to the many events of life and never taking a moment to pause or reflect. Always late and rarely on time. Maybe we got this from the corporate world. Run around the office with lots of papers, a phone to your ear, and lots of excel files open on your desktop (because excel files are big and scary and contain lots of numbers and things). That says you are a hard worker.

Hero: Unrealized Value

Subconsciously we think, if I am busy, then I must be productive. Busyness doesn't build talent, it only fuels fear. It may be possible that some seasons demand more than others. That is natural. Knowing what you are fit to do rather than doing what you fit in your schedule becomes the key.

Quit sooner and do what is most critical to the direction your life is set to go. You will realize the unrealized potential you have.

9. The Fear of the Unknown

This fear is labeled as the ultra-planner. The underlining pattern of thinking goes like this: If I know, then I am in control. This makes it very difficult to deviate from the plan.

Don't get me wrong. Planning is critical. Trying to use a plan to control circumstances that no longer make sense is what makes plans a challenge.

This fear makes people uncomfortable with risk: financial risk, social interactions, and life's new seasons. Most of the time, this fear is demonstrated in a habit of overestimating risk and overlooking benefits.

Hero: Peace

Can you stick with the calling while changing up the plan? Can you uphold your internal freedom in a world of uncertainty? When plans change, can you readjust quickly? Because, as we know, uncertainty will never go away. What is true, however, is that we can learn to take this natural part of life at a much calmer level. To have peace in the midst of uncertainty is a powerful trait of God.

10. The Fear of Being Passionless

This fear asks you: will you ever find your calling? When someone is passionate about something—maybe it is a relief effort, a vision for a business, a creative pursuit, or even the story of Jesus, your fear of that person's passion may make you write them off. You may want to defend the status quo or think that they are too passionate. The world will discourage this 'abnormal' behavior. When this fear is in control, its worst feature is when we come to terms with it agenda. That is, this fear will tell you it's okay to settle, be average, and live a deferred life plan. When passion comes close to the fear of being passionless, the fear will tell you, thank you, but no thank you. Keep that to yourself.

Heroine: Devotion

Can you do something in spite of fear? Your passion is your connection to living life. It is your devotion.

Devote yourself to what you feel is most important despite what people say. This is not selfish. Whether it is to be a preacher, a butcher, a creative, a business leader, a world traveler, a writer, a missionary, a doctor, a music expert, or a nurse, devote yourself to it. Who knows, maybe one day that thing that you are afraid to be passionate about will be the very thing that gives your life more meaning. If He called you to do it, He will supply you with the power necessary to achieve it.

To chase your dreams, chase your fears.

Right now, I want you to write down in less than two minutes your top five fears. If this is your first time or tenth time reading this book, I want you to do this task with the same intensity. Write down your top five fears. Just jot down five, now.

Keep that note or piece of paper, we will need it later.

Your Most Ambitious Goal

I know God won't give me anything I can't handle. I just wish he didn't trust me so much.

MOTHER TERESA, NOBEL PEACE PRIZE LAUREATE

During one point of this manuscript, I did a bit of market research. I sent out a survey. I asked twelve friends a list of questions to help define profiles for the readership. It would help me define relevant issues, challenges, and desires. In each survey, I asked: What is your most ambitious goal?

Every response was different. Here are a few:
- To serve others—at work, in a hospital, or as a missionary
- To inspire others
- To have a great family
- To be a light to those in my sphere of influence
- To create
- To shape culture
- To start a business that helps tons of people

What I soon came to realize, as they were all different, they all had one underlining theme. They were all very selfless goals.

There is an incredible part of us, deep down, that connects our most ambitious goal to giving. Giving is an act much bigger than ourselves. It's something we desire to do.

In essence, we want to love and serve others. My hope is that by the time you finish this book, you discover your ability to transform your life in hopes that you can love and serve others.

Unfortunately, very few will actualize this heart. Most people don't give their ambitious goal the attention it needs. Often, it's that we neglect our hearts most ambitious goal for some level of fear or hesitation.

All the while, the folks around us are suffering. From a neighbor who can't give up his alcohol addiction to people hundreds of miles away being displaced from their country. The label refugee makes me cringe. I think of those trapped in North Korea today who live under extremely difficult circumstances. Some work sixteen plus hours a day digging for food in the trash so they can feed their families. Oh, and they are only children.[1]

I think of the stateless Rohingya Muslim population in Southeast Asia who has been thrown into concentration camps, today, in our modern world. Children who are being beaten and then sold as human labor throughout Thailand, Malaysia, and Indonesia. Their rights have been taken from them, their families are unable to seek medical care in an emergency. They are encamped, unable to leave their detestable quarters. In early 2016, the population of about 1.4 million Rohingya Muslims in Myanmar (formerly known as Burma) are the most persecuted people group in the world.

Whatever your most ambitious goal - to be an entrepreneur, a world traveler, a family man, a leader, or a light to your sphere of influence—the journey to become your best self begins with knowing where you are right now. You will have to work on developing yourself to reach your most ambitious goal. It is not only a question of what you need to do but who you need to become.

These nine persona's below outline the starting point for many:

The Seeker

You currently are doing ministry. You love God and believe in God yet lack purpose in your day-to-day affairs. You aren't sure exactly where you want to go. And sometimes, all you know is that you don't want to be where you are now.

The Prodigy

Your parents gave up a lot and also envisioned a big future for you.

As you get older, the vision they had does not seem to be panning out the way they wanted it to. They said a happy, full life for you is to be a doctor or a lawyer. That is how you become a provider for your family and buy a nice home.

But, when you look at their formula for a happy life, you see gaps.

This aged, almost dried-up way of thinking represents everything that is wrong with the world. Not that their intentions are bad. No, I apologize if you thought that. No, it is just that your battles are different from theirs.

As it seems, we recklessly abandon our father's wisdom, our mother's path and we become the modern day prodigy turned prodigal.

The Lover

Maybe you had a love. You became friends, then, in a few dreamy weeks, you find yourself together.

A few years go by.

Then, suddenly, as you try over and over to win his heart, he abandons the relationship. What was so easily kindled before was getting more frustrating to even maintain. Despite all the heartache and the fights and long nights, you would do anything to somehow stay bonded.

Ruined by this, you will do anything to get him back. You are happiest with him and are left where the entire story began: alone and searching.

All the while, you keep trying to persuade yourself to look forward when really you are stuck looking back. You don't see how you can be happy again without him. The only way now to move forward is to leave your other half behind and recreate yourself... again.

The Carefree

Maybe everything was going right, but suddenly the party came to an end. The crowds disappeared and you were left wondering: what is next? Alone at a major crossroads you must choose which way to go. Is the dream over? Have you learned or gained anything?

The Predestined

Raised with everything you could dream of having, you are content.

Friends say you are lucky. A beautiful family, house, and the opportunity of your future glows bright. Your parents are well-respected by their peers. You are rich with knowledge. You have seen the world, experienced being in the presence of the wealthy and powerful.

But, as you have never felt life's fundamental struggle around shelter and food, you battle internally to make your life meaningful. This bleeds into your relationships and decisions. Deep down, you keep asking: how do I make my life meaning-full?

The Rebel

At one end stands the unrelenting father, demanding his position as head of the household, no matter what the cost. The agenda seems to be outdated. Especially when it means you cannot do what you want to do.

On the other hand, you, a young individual, who sets out with hopes and dreams to be a better balance of compassion and strength, you still have a major set of obstacles to overcome with no example to learn from. Deep down you represent all that life is—expansion in an ever constricting world. Your challenge: finding the balance of love and strength.

The Idealist

You were brought up in Sunday school and summer vacation Bible school programs. Overtime, as you get older, you lost track of what was routine and what was relational. Now, you search for a faith. A faith you want to call your own. An authentic life is one where you can pen your future and feel confident in your choices.

The Creator

You are done wandering through the world hoping for something to turn up.

Everyone is a creator. You, however, have an explicitly strong passion to bring into reality things that alter the status quo of daily life. You want to shape your story, as much as you look for a greater sense of purpose and calling to live for.

The Regular

Things are going well and promises of hope for the future shine bright. Your first choice college accepted you (plus three additional schools most people only dream about attending). You are working a great job after college. Suddenly, something enters your life that threatens all stability and completeness.

Everything that was at it should be, begins to be as it shouldn't. The great schooling, the elite job, and even the paycheck all seem to be there. You find yourself in a place where meaning is lacking. Hardship comes and you are utterly broken due to the fact that you have no idea why you should persevere. You ask yourself, "What is my life about?" Everything on the outside is just right, but inside it seems off.*

One Caveat: You may read this and say: I really don't fit into any type of groups. You may feel zero connection with one of the personas. Even if problems may not exist now, this is the best time to start preparing. When the pressure of life is not on, when the world is not demanding but gently asking you to be stronger, to be bigger, to stand taller, don't underestimate the power of preparation.

What plot is shaping your narrative? In a life of constant flux, each day throws us new challenges. These personas could either be the doorpost to freedom or the weight of imprisonment. Identify the narrative above (circle it, write it, pick your top three) that is shaping your story. It's the starting point to know where you are going.

The Call—The Power of Young People

Never tell a young person that anything cannot be done. God may have been waiting centuries for someone ignorant enough of the impossible to do that very thing.

G. M. TREVELYAN, BRITISH HISTORIAN AND AUTHOR

Young people make up billion dollar industries. Think of Snapchat. Young people have the ability to change habits easily. Young people can give up their whole lives for Christ quickly, with lots of vulnerability and lots of vigor. Young people are able to learn from the older generation about life, work, and God's faithfulness. There are over seven billion people on the planet. And just in the last few years, the statistics show that more than half of those people are under the age of thirty.[1] That's 3,500,000,000+ people! Young people can start movements and trends that change the world.

In the Middle East, dictatorship and political corruption propelled young people to use social media to spark the Arab Spring. In Southeast Asia, college students looking for freedom began to hold peaceful rallies against twenty-five years of a repressive military regime. They started an election process that last for another twenty-five years. In 2010, after fifty years of tyranny, the grips of a military junta began to loosen. In Hong Kong, young people are fighting for democracy. All these events have happened recently. The power of young people makes me think:

What if nothing stood in your way of discovering your true-self, today? What if, you realized you are more powerful than you knew? How would that impact the world?

Person-Specific Purpose

A Lockheed F-22 Raptor jets top speed is nearly 1,500 mph. As it flies through the air it can become invisible to enemy radar. Imagine you flew that F-22 jet with clear blue skies and no clouds in sight. You are captain of the best jet ever built. You knew that when it was time for your mission, you were equipped, ready, and mighty.

Now image the F-22 is your character. In the same way that it seems like nothing could hold back the Raptor jet, your character was never set up to hold you back. You are made with ultimate precision, care, and hustle. What if nothing restricted you? What if nothing stood in your way of achieving your goals?

What if you had the freedom to be yourself in a world burdened by people-pleasing, social pressure, self-doubt, apathy, and fear? When the call comes, you believe in yourself, you initiate, and bring into reality what was only a vision.

Eudaimonia, according to the Greeks, is a state of 'human flourishing.' It's similar to the phrase the sky's the limit. It's the point of reaching your ultimate best. It some ways, it's like the F-22. You are reaching your full potential.

The challenge is living out our person-specific purpose.
We live out the gospel in direct proportion to how clearly we see it spelled out in every detail of life. If we cannot 'see' the gospel in our classroom, our workplace, or our neighborhood, we struggle to live it out with intentionality. If we cannot see our purpose in 2016, 2018, and 2022, we will struggle to be everything God made us to be.

What if, as you read this call on your life, as a young, inexperienced individual you answer wholeheartedly, fully-invested, and commit to work on your purpose every day?

The Bible tells us that we are given purpose in our life. That means your time on this earth is valuable. That means your time on this earth has a cause. That means your purpose is yours and you must discover it. You are made to grow, expand, stretch, and develop throughout life. It also means that you have an obligation to bring about something while you are here.

I believe that for every young individual reading this book you're furnished with all the proper tools to accomplish your purpose, dreams, and desires. The beauty comes when you believe in yourself and continue, despite any setback, to move forward. To continue to write if publishers deny you. To continue to sing even when only family and friends listen. To continue to progress in whatever you have been given, whether people applaud you or not.

That is, Purpose. Built. Young.

Accept, as I do, all the hardship that faithfulness to the Gospel entails in the strength that God gives you. For he has rescued us from all that is really evil and called us to a life of holiness—not because of any of our achievements but for his own purpose.

Second Epistle to Timothy 1:8b-9
J.B. Phillips New Testament (PHILLIPS)

Don't Get Lured by the Gingerbread (Definition of Success)

**Try not to become a man of success,
but rather try to become a man of value.**

ALBERT EINSTEIN, A PIONEER PHYSICIST

In a big city, there were once two innocent young children. They were thrown out into the world to care for themselves. Orphaned by bad parents, they had no other choice but to fend for themselves. They circled around the cold streets of the big city, each day, only to find their hunger ever-present. One day, their appetite began waning away when a lovely old lady offered them some gingerbread cookies.

If they would only come into the old lady's house, she would serve them hot, freshly baked gingerbread delights. For these children, who hadn't eaten anything decent in days, each morsel, without a doubt, carried the delight of a thousand meals.

They took the offer, gladly.

Unexpectedly, they came to find this lady was cruel.

She imprisoned the children.

They got lured by the gingerbread.

The gingerbread delights were only a quick-fix to a bigger and wider dilemma.

How do you define success (the gingerbread cookies of your life)? Not in your job, not in your relationship. But in your life? How will you gauge your success?

There are many different things we can substitute for God. Each morsel, without a doubt, carries the delight of one thousand meals. We will call them the 3P's. The world's definition of success usually falls somewhere in between these three categories: position, power, and possessions. Here are three critical questions around the typical definition of success we should answer. To make these relevant, I have included real life examples:

Position: Why can Michael Phelps gain great position—the world's top Olympic athlete—and not consider himself just an athlete?

Power: Why can Ernest Hemingway obtain great power and yet not believe in himself?

Possessions: Why can Adolf Merckle possess great wealth—the richest German in the modern era, able to buy a new car, a beautiful home, and travel anywhere in the world— still not be able to reinvent himself after failure?

Let's break down each separately.

Position

In an article posted by Sports Illustrated, a headshot of Michael Phelps on the cover showed a rugged and transformed Phelps. Wearing a white tee-shirt, he appears to have had a complete renewal.

But, from what?

The first P: Position

After winning twenty-two medals over an eight year span, Phelps was on the brink of devastation. He had dealt with a drinking problem, a world of doubt in himself, and a few relationships that had gone wrong. It wasn't just a scandal of smoking marijuana that put him into a state of inner turmoil.

Deep down, he had mistakenly avoided confronting his fears. He could not handle the bareness of himself alone. His public image was all he had come to know of himself.

"I wound up uncovering a lot of things about myself, "Phelps said in the interview for Sports Illustrated. "For a long time, I saw myself as the athlete that I was, but not as a human being." He had won eight gold medals in 2008 alone. He was one of the world's top athletes. No one as spectacular as Phelps has ever competed in the Olympics. He surpassed some of the highest levels of human achievement at an alarmingly high-rate.

The danger of believing in the first P: position, a highly sought-after gingerbread cookie, is this: Why can a man of world class athletics not consider himself just an athlete (or a doctor, entrepreneur, or high-level manager)?

Power

Then there is the second P: Power

The story is so familiar and distasteful. People are elevated into a place of power. They have millions of followers around the world. Then, out of the blue, the news reports of their death. Whitney Houston, a best-selling music artist, at age forty-eight. Amy Winehouse, joining the "Twenty-seven club" was a five-time Grammy award winner, at age twenty-seven. Robin Williams, a worldwide known comedian, known for making people laugh, at age sixty-three. A common thread in each scenario was a lack of belief in oneself.

After achieving heights that most dream about and tasting the best gingerbread cookies life can offer, something was still missing inside.

Harper Lee, after writing To Kill A Mockingbird, spent years away from writing. Could she top her last work? She struggled with picking up a pen all because of the fame of To Kill a Mockingbird. Ernest Hemingway struggled with his own self-image. Both were considered timeless authors. Why couldn't their writing (or their songs or Grammys or movies) sustain them?

Why can an individual obtain great power and yet still not believe in themselves?

Possessions

Then there is the third P: Possessions

Finally, the story does not change for those who garner the most coveted prize of all, the third P: Possessions. Adolf Merckle, one of the richest men in Germany's history, was sitting on a fortune of billions of dollars. His conglomerate of companies - he had built during his lifetime - made him the richest man in Germany in 2007.

When he began his career, he took over a family business of eighty employees and turned it into a 30-billion-euro empire. A self-made man indeed. With money like that, his power and position came from his wealth. He ranked in the top one hundred richest people in the world.

After the 2008 crash, his net worth was at risk of being lost. He approached a few banks to get loans to cover his debt. At the time, banks were afraid to lend money. Many rejected him.

On January 5, 2009, Mr. Merckle left home to head to the office. He found a nearby train station and waited, not on the platform, but on the tracks. That day he committed suicide.

To everyone's surprise, a few days later, a bank offered the right amount of funds needed for a loan.

Why can a man like Adolf Merckle have the keys to the world (to purchase a new car, a new house, or a new outfit), still feel unable to start again anew? To reinvent himself? What does a billionaire who finds a fifty percent loss in net worth lack that he must kill himself?

Uncovered Gingerbread Cookies

People chase the 3P's (the gingerbread cookies of life) for what is behind them.

Respect. Notoriety. Feeling loved. Accepted. Revered.

And frankly, the 3P's are not bad. Michael Phelps, Ernest Hemingway, and Adolf Merckle are not bad people. We are all just as susceptible to define success by the 3P's. It's what people demonstrate (the lack of character) that causes pain and destruction around the 3P's. That is why we cannot define success by them. It's much better we define success by something solid. We must have a better approach to success, the Pioneer Approach.

Nothing can withstand the power of the human will if it is willing to stake its very existence to the extent of its purpose.

Benjamin Disraeli
Former Prime Minister of the United Kingdom

The Pioneer Approach

What you do with what you have, despite the harshest of circumstances, builds a pioneer.

DAVID ISKANDER

Prime Delivery of $1 Million

Amazon Prime recently introduced one-hour delivery in my city.

One day, I was at work and I began to ask people this question: If you had $1 million given to you in the next five minutes, and had one hour to spend it, what would you spend it on? And in one hour, any remaining money would be wiped out of your account, for good. You lose it. What would you buy?

Now, the only rule I gave them was they cannot put it in a bank account or buy stocks or bonds or invest it. You have to spend it. What would you get? Oh, and, if you are wondering... you can buy property.

Before you move ahead, think or write your answer.

One person explained to me how they would strategically set up requirements for their family to fulfill. If they fulfilled the requirements, each family member would get a portion. I don't think he would make the hour cut off time.

I had another person tell me that they would give half of it away to a charity and the other half toward traveling the world. They would have to book a lot of flights quick!

I had someone else tell me that they would buy a house, get a new car, and quit their job.

But the most resounding answer was something I didn't expect.

To the over fifty people I asked, the majority of people said they would give $500K to charity and spend the other $500K on themselves (and family). People literally divided up their tax free earnings to charity and personal use.

I was surprised.

The answer should reflect how you utilize your resources, time, and energy right now. Think about it, you have been given a "$1 Million Account" that must be spent by the time you step into heaven. What you do with your resources in life are reflective of your true answer.

What makes this little nonofficial research study so insightful is that people said they would give away half the money. When time was limited, what people would do with their resources changed dramatically from what they currently do every day.

This did make me happy, though. People genuinely want to love and serve more. If they felt they could and understood the brevity of life, then they would give more. If they felt the strength of a limited amount of time, they may in fact open up to giving half of their time and energy to others. Because, when there isn't much time, focusing only on ourselves gets boring quick.

And this is the beauty of the Pioneer Approach and the ultimate goal that we have to love and serve others, radically. This approach has the power to turn your agenda from self-service to selfless-service. Namely, the Pioneer Approach makes your reality a Kingdom-centered plan.

The Pioneer Approach is to build
- character that utilizes surrounding resources to draw a high-return,
- character that can withstand the ebbs and flows of commissary life, and
- character that can love and serve its sphere of influence, radically.

Let's break each one down separately.

Goal #1: Resourcefulness

Build character that utilizes surrounding resources to draw a high-return.
To be a pioneer, one must be resourceful. Malcolm Gladwell in his book Outliers makes this statement: "Outliers are those who have been given opportunities- and who have had the strength and presence of mind to seize them." In other words, he concludes that success is highly influenced by a resourceful person. One must have the audacity to look at harsh circumstances, still believe and utilize their resources to draw a high-return.

How can a group of high school students in Torrance, California feed thousands of people for Christmas, cloth hundreds of orphans, and save over 700 lives by donating blood?

Resourcefulness.

By collecting food cans, donating used clothing, and providing blood for others, a group of fourteen to eighteen year olds are able to impact thousands of people all around the world.

Is it because they are the wealthiest? Nope.

Resourcefulness is a mindset of how one is equipped, not necessarily an accumulation of things.

Most will think of a pioneer as a person of great adventure, exploration, and ingenuity. When in fact, it is much more about what you do with what you have. A pioneer takes the opportunity of life and brings back a high-return.

The next challenge is the obligation of daily life.

Goal #2: Commissary Life

Build character that can withstand the ebbs and flows of commissary life.
Your commissary life is simply your day-to-day obligations mixed with your calling.

We have our responsibilities (pay for school, rent, and our phone bill) plus bringing our calling to life, in every season. Sometimes this is easy. Other times, the ebbs and flows weigh heavy. When we know we have a special reason for existing, other people are depending on us, and we have been entrusted from a higher power, we learn how to withstand the ebbs and flows with consistency. Admittedly, we face a great host of challenges that conspire against us chasing our calling. It's just like the uncontrollable wind a Raptor jet must face. Commissary life is taking care of your responsibility while never diminishing or disaffirming your calling.

You may want to be a photographer. Your parents are telling you that you must go to college and study something that will make you money. So, as you don't want to get kicked out, you are taking courses at community college. You know for sure that there is nothing more that you love than to take photos (or at least, that is what you believe now). So, how do you bring that about? You equip yourself to handle the ebbs and flows, the good and bad in each season, to achieve your goals, no matter what. If we don't begin to intentionally make space for our calling, life is easily jam-packed with things outside our calling.

Being able to withstand the ebbs and flows of our commissary life expound one main point: never let your present circumstances lessen the power of your calling .

Goal #3: Love and Service, Radically

Build character that can love and serve its sphere of influence, radically.
This is our overarching mandate. To be able to love and serve, radically, in everything we do is a powerful accomplishment. It happens once people begin to capitalize on the first two goals.

Primarily, our sphere of influence is no longer based on geographic proximity. That it, it is no longer based on your city. Can you build a relationship with people that relate to you from around the world? Your life can span oceans, government regulations, and cultural barriers. My family is originally from Egypt. My uncle spends time during his week on an online chat. He has the opportunity, as he speaks Arabic, to preach the Gospel to people throughout the Middle East. He is able to see people come to Christ that he has never met.

Today, your community is defined as the group of people you choose to connect with.

Let's look at the value of love and service individually.

Love

Love...interrupts at every hour the most serious occupations, and sometimes perplexes for a while even the greatest minds. It does not hesitate... to interfere with the negotiations of statesmen and the investigations of the learned. It knows how to slip its love-notes and ringlets even into ministerial portfolios and philosophical manuscripts... It sometimes demands the sacrifice of...health, sometimes of wealth, position and happiness.
ARTHUR SCHOPENHAUER, GERMAN PHILOSOPHER

The power of love is to fundamentally change someone for the better. The deeper the love, the deeper the impact.

In Myanmar, I have partnered with a network of orphanages. The network began with one couple, Pastor Peter and Rebecca. They had a deep desire to combat orphan vulnerability. At the time when they were thinking of beginning the orphanage, the country was under heavy military rule. Resources were limited, and the future was highly uncertain.

They were a young couple and had no idea what God had in store for them. They began the orphanage in 1995 called Love Children's Home (www.LoveChildrensHome.org) with about twenty children in a bamboo hut. They started small, but that did not mean that they were not strong.

They did a great job of pouring deep love into the children. Namely, deep love by caring for the children's needs, physically and spiritually.

In 2016, Pastor Peter has now helped over 1000 orphans. Plus, some of the first orphans that he and Rebecca cared for twenty years ago are starting their own orphanages! This radical love started by one couple was able to transform the lives of many.

It is easy to overlook humble beginnings. Starting an orphanage is hard work. Starting an orphanage under a heavy military rule is even harder. And, starting an orphanage under heavy military rule that opposes Christianity, now that is unrealistic... unless love is at the center.

Never underestimate your ability to love.

Service

"Learn to do more for people, than anyone else. It is not what we get. But who we become, what we contribute... that gives meaning to our lives."
TONY ROBBINS, AUTHOR, PHILANTHROPIST, AND SPEAKER

Genuine service seeks to gain nothing in return. It is Jesus-living. It's how he defined greatness. Service responds out of gratitude toward life. It does not matter where you are in life; service is something you can do every day. Charles Spurgeon gave us this example:

Once upon a time there was a gardener who grew an enormous carrot. He took it to his king and said, "My lord, this is the greatest carrot I've ever grown or ever will grow; therefore, I want to present it to you as a token of my love and respect for you." The king was touched and discerned the man's heart, so as he turned to go, the king said, "Wait! You are clearly a good steward of the earth. I own a plot of land right next to yours. I want to give it to you freely as a gift, so you can garden it all." The gardener was amazed and delighted and went home rejoicing. But there was a nobleman at the king's court who overheard all this, and he said, "My! If that is what you get for a carrot, what if you gave the king something better?" The next day the nobleman came before the king, and he was leading a handsome black stallion. He bowed low and said, "My lord, I breed horses, and this is the greatest horse I've ever bred or ever will; therefore, I want to present it to you as a token of my love and respect for you." But the king discerned his heart and said, "Thank you," and took the horse and simply dismissed him. The nobleman was perplexed, so the king said, "Let me explain. That gardener was giving me the carrot, but you were giving yourself the horse."

Give carrots, not horses. We have no idea the ripple effect caused by the service we initiate in our lives. Imagine with me for a moment that just one act of kindness in your sphere of influence can affect hundreds of thousands of people. Your good deed can produce a collection of good deeds to pass on to others.

Winning the lottery won't make you more generous. Your limited capacity will make you more generous. Giving up your time, energy, and resources for others in the middle of a commissary lifestyle is an opportunity for true blessing.

Give, and know that giving is better than receiving.

The way the Pioneer Approach redefines success challenges what the world calls ultimate satisfaction. This definition of success redefines many of the almost inherent beliefs we have about success. In all situations, the 3P's won't cut it close. Rarely, do we do our best work when our ambitions and drive are set on fulfilling only our own selves. When we consider the community at large, whatever community that is, we take on a type of energy that can create a future engine that will pull us toward the goal despite any setbacks.

> Here is a quick assignment: Check yourself against the $1 million question. Is what you do with your resources—time, energy, and purpose—reflective of what you believe?
> If you see a discrepancy in your answer and your life, you have something worth working toward. Compared to the success of the world, this is a great gauge of what we truly value and what we want to do.

In any case, to have a radical shift in our life toward the Pioneer Approach, we must start from the ground up. That is, we must go to the core of our being, our heart.

καρδία (Kardia): The Heart's Desire

There is not one of these transformations in which the heart is left without an object. Its desire for one particular object may be conquered; but as to its desire for having some one object or other, this is unconquerable

THOMAS CHALMERS IN *THE EXPULSIVE POWER OF A NEW AFFECTION*

In Greek, kardia represents the heart. In every single reference in the Bible (some 800+ times), the word never actually refers to your physical heart. Rather, kardia denotes your inner being.

And with this in mind, today the heart is easily ignored. There isn't much pressure in life to actively change the heart. We point out people's shortcomings, but rarely speak to their hearts. There is more pressure for someone to eat a second slice of cake than to develop one's heart. In other words, because it's easier to find something to rate (like getting hired, losing 15 pounds, or getting married) than developing the right heart (knowing God as provider, your source of strength, or building your faith), many default to what's simpler.

And the Bible is very clear: your heart matters most to God1.

If you overlook your core, your progress will always be stunted. It's like looking at the height of a plant and wanting it to grow taller, but it can't because the pot it is in has limited space for the roots to grow.

How do you measure your progress toward having the right heart?

Kardia Expounded

The heart is...
The core of every human being.
The most essential and formative part of an individual.
The deepest depths.
Without the heart, the individual is lifeless.
The heart is where a disease takes place and healing occurs.
The heart is where unity is built and jealousy is brewed.
The heart is the province where true life and death—light and darkness—campaign against each other.
The heart is what Jesus wants from us more than our actions, our deeds, or our ability.
The fruits of the Spirit are a byproduct of a right heart stance.
Faith is a rendezvous between God and your heart and your heart and your actions.
That is, your heart is what connects your actions to God and God to your actions.
Your heart tells if you truly care for people or yourself within one single action.
The inner life of a person is embodied in the heart.
What you do habitually is a reflection of what your heart values.
It's where pride and servant-hood are contained.
It is the essential core of every human being.
It is something we never see but through the reflection of action.
It is the fundamental core of any individual.

The Gospels and the Heart

When Jesus fed 5000 people, He addressed a heart issue, not a food issue. When the disciples commented about not having enough food, Jesus confronted their hearts about God supplying all their needs. Rather than complain about them, he told them to thank God for what little they did have.

When Jesus healed the sick, He confronts the heart condition of faith. Many of the times he healed, He asked if they believed, because healing is much more about believing than healing. Jesus loves his children to be healthy physically, but more importantly, spiritually healthy.

Every action and word Jesus speaks in the Bible confronts a heart condition.

Our hearts are the focal point of how we see what happens in our life and what we choose to do, in any given circumstance. T. D. Jakes said, "If you got life on the inside, then death on the outside won't stop you from living. In fact, it will fertilize what God has put down inside of you."

What if, in the middle of being fired, being dumped, or being unwanted, your calling reveals itself the brightest? When everything is trying to destroy you, the one thing that will keep you alive, your inner strength, will reveal itself. It becomes the only thing that you can continue to persevere to do. That is, when everything fails around you, Jesus doesn't. This is the power of a strong heart.

Just like gold being tested by fire, all the dirt goes to the surface, and at the core, the gold is purest.

What Your Heart Desires

Cleansing the heart takes a constant internal awareness of its current position.

Thomas Chalmer outlines this very well in *The Expulsive Power of a New Affection:*

"It is seldom that any of our bad habits or flaws disappears by mere process of natural extinction. At least it is very seldom that that this is done through the instrumentality of reasoning or by the force of mental determination. But what cannot be destroyed can be dispossessed."

What Chalmers so clearly points to is that the heart desires an object. Just like a home, the heart will always have a tenant (desire). Desire is permanent. He doesn't ever leave. He can never be removed.

You will desire something. The call you have been given is to bring forth your full potential of your desire.

This is why, once you are born again (completely renewed in spirit), you must canvas the property of your heart to dispose of any harmful elements. It takes time to transform into Godly-quality.

I remember when I first got saved, I was leaving church on fire. It was so energizing for me. I would get in my car and start bumping vulgar rap music. Literally, I was blasting it through the church parking lot. I soon realized that this probably wasn't congruent with my new spirit.

Rather than trying to destroy a heart's desire, we must evict it. The way to do that is to replace it.

Instead of Nipsey Hussle, I started listening to Lecrae.

To expose and evict a bad habit, it must be replaced with something—a good habit, a new belief, a new thought, a truth statement. Often times, one begins to overcome this conflict when they confront their thinking about the conflict. For instance, one can go from, "I can never do a project so well" to "I have everything I need to make this happen." Or, "I don't have enough time to pray and read my Bible" to "I will have enough time to pray and read my Bible."

Developing godly character creates a highly spiritual individual and is your highest responsibility.

Your Highest Responsibility

Your highest ethical responsibility is to make sure your life aligns with your purpose. Anything less is a misuse of your most valuable resources.

Your relationships, your inspiration to others, and your ability to shape culture all come from YOUR heart stance.

That is worth repeating: your relationships, your creative power, your inspiration to others, your service to others, your marriage, your ability to shape culture are all contingent on your heart stance. It's what God cares about most.

So if your heart is so important, what do we do when there is something that we like to change? Build character.

God's Plan for Your Life?

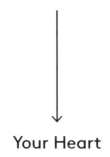

Your Heart

And Then What?

Whatever. You. Want.
(Because if He has your heart, you will want
whatever He wants)

Life Constriction 1: Social Terrain

The surest way to corrupt a youth is to instruct him to hold in higher esteem those who think alike than those who think differently.

FRIEDRICH NIETZSCHE, PHILOSOPHER

Meet Dan

Dan is a 19-year-old college student going to a major private university. Dan is paying some $35k a year for his education. Well, he agreed to pay someone back.

Dan is a bright kid. He has a good head on his shoulders.

He is unsure of what he wants to do with his future. Dan's issue? He is spending $35k a year to go to school, he is not sure what he wants to do, his parents (whether he knows it or not) are a big part of the decision for him to go to college.

Dan now realizes that he must move out. How is Dan supposed to go to college, live on his own, and afford food on $12 an hour?

Meet Dan's Friends

Dan has a friend named Laura. Laura is in the same boat, practically. Although, Laura knows what she wants, she is struggling to make it happen. She really wants to work with digital art.

Laura is out of her wits on how to make it happen. Her parents worked typical jobs for their entire careers. She feels unsure of what to do.

Then there is Tim, Dan's best friend. Tim is all together a moral compass in Dan's life. But Tim, he seems to have created a bunch of awesome ideas, but has no idea how to execute.

"I am still young (19 years old), I have never done it before, and I can do it after college," he tells himself. His lack of experience is costing him time, passion, and resources that he won't have after graduation.

The Social Terrain

Our surroundings, what we call our Social Terrain, has more influence on our future than we realize.

Imagine sitting in the middle of a trampoline or a giant bounce house. The surface of the trampoline or bounce house bends toward us as if everything around is putting extra pressuring on us.

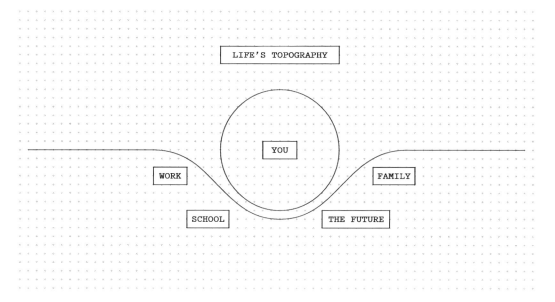

Visual 3
Life has a trampoline effect.
As Einstein first postulated
that space can bend,
our lives have a way
of being directly pressured
by our surroundings.

It's hard to imagine dropping your first EP when you are working a minimum wage job. Your environment doesn't reflect who you want to become. Nor does it care. It pressures you to live a certain way—whether that is in your interest of your purpose or not.

This is true for the inexperienced preacher whose parents want him to get a real degree. Or the recent graduate with $20K of school loans who is trying to figure out what she wants to do with the rest of her life.

Our Social Terrain, wherever we live and work, dictates a lot of our actions consciously and subconsciously. The challenge is that decisions we make can place more value on the path of least resistance over purpose.

Parents used to worry about their kids in high school succumbing to peer pressure like drinking and smoking. Now that social pressure is just as relevant in terms of the education we pursue, the vocation we choose, the risks we take, and assuredly the purpose we live out. To embrace our Social Terrain and make it gospel positioned, we have to understand all the different forces around us that have the ability to shape our decision-making.

There are four major parts to our Social Terrain that have the most power of shaping our future. Namely, the education system, our career choices, social pressure, and risk.

The key is realizing that the pressure of the Social Terrain will always be there. And as complex as it sounds, rather than being overwhelmed by it, we can shape it.

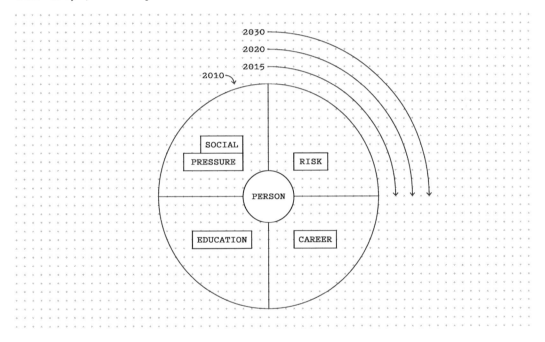

Education

College, what was supposed to free us and give us the option to choose any career path we desire, is no longer the key to a successful career.

For many, college is indebted them to student loan payments for twenty years post-graduation. Want to take a gap year, travel, and learn more about who you are as an individual? Want to have more time to explore (than just two weeks a year)? The only option is to wait for another forty years.

As we saw earlier, a job today in the corporate world offers no more security than a car with its doors locked and windows down.

Visual 4: The Social Terrain
The Social Terrain is constantly changing.
Each year it is in motion.
Sometimes these categorizes affect us more or less in particular seasons.

Career

Many careers built in the name of lifestyle goals have become an most infectious trap.

Is it possible to do a job you love that is not an escape from your real life?

For many, the corporate system is a prison sentence.

A concentration camp is defined briefly as a persecuted minority, deliberately imprisoned, with inadequate facilities.

Many, not all, corporate career paths are luxurious slave camps. They offer retirement plans, 'benefits,' and even the occasional office lunch. But, in exchange for what?

You may have nice bathrooms, nice conference rooms, a nice kitchen even. Do you have space to pray, relax your eyes for thirty minutes, or simply go for a walk? The corporate world has the better end of the bargain. They gain all of the benefits while we inherit the infectious trap of a mortgage, car payment, and don't forget, student loans.

Social Pressure

One major social pressure is the generational social pressure that demands outdated practices on new times. Not in values but in tactics. For instance, the old narrative that college would guarantee a job is gone. Yet, somehow so many high school graduates end up in a college classroom stacking up loans, while being unsure of what they want to do next. Is this because job descriptions require a four-year degree? What would happen if that requirement went away? Would college be less necessary?

A fascinating example comes from the likes of the British aristocracy that ruled for 1,000 years over the United Kingdom and, at one point, the majority of the world.

During the establishment of British rule, the Kingdom established a system to protect wealth and inheritance. Rightfully so, as these families were disproportionally wealthy. They established the hierarchy of who would receive the wealth as members of the royal family passed away.

At one point it made sense. This was a wise decision.

Not too much later, say maybe only about one hundred years ago, things began to shift.

Because the laws made it clear who would receive the inheritance – the position, the power, and the possessions – children happily would marry into other royal families. This further protected the inheritance.

They just happened to forget about one important aspect: love.

Soon, newly engaged couples were talking more about love than comparing estates. They were more concerned with how they were going to live together. This began to disrupt the practice of the previous generations. The times had changed. The world had changed. Yet, the social pressure of British rule had not.

The original intentions of the British rulers made sense when they established the rules. Yet, over time, things simply changed.

Today we see young people upset that their work is unfulfilled. We see a generation above us who worked with strong conviction and loyalty to a company. They teach us to do the same. For our parents, their original hope was to provide stability for a family. I am personally so thankful for this.

Now, many young adults are not just asking for stability, but purpose. A job we love. The same way love became a key element in the future of the aristocracy, purpose is also becoming a key note in the way we make decisions.

Another major social pressure is the question we dislike hearing and yet still resort to when we meet someone new.

"Hi!, What is your name?," the new acquaintance asks.

My name is _____, you answer.

"What do you do?," they ask.

Internally, you begin to bicker and scream and yell and fight them. But, you just met them. So you decide to be polite. You answer in the most socially acceptable way. A freelancer, a designer, a student. Or, you refrain from answering in great detail. I work full-time.

I remember meeting someone that, as soon as they were asked this question, they closed their eyes, tilted their head back, and sighed.

Isn't it interesting that, when you are asked what you do for a living and the answer you give is "work a full-time job," you have told them nothing of what you actually do? Often, this question devalues us and makes us feel like we are only what we do. As if our current job situation reflects our value.

For about five years now, I have worked with orphans in Myanmar bringing support, aid, and teams to the orphanage. Since my first experience in the beautiful and cultured city of Yangon, I learned something profound that many people will see but seldom understand. Namely, a rich life has nothing to do with stuff.

The children have stories of being abandoned by their parents: their parents died or were too poor to care for them. So, they brought them to the orphanage. At the orphanage, the children have two outfits and sleep in bamboo makeshift homes. These children may have one meal a day.

There are rarely enough care takers. Therefore, only so much love and attention can go around.

The weather in Myanmar is extreme. For one season, the weather is just awfully hot. It's hard to do anything active. The shaded concrete is hard to walk on. The kids are not allowed to play and it is unbearable for a person who has never experienced it. For another season, it is extremely rainy and humid. You put on a jacket to shield from the rain. As soon as you walk outside, you want to take off the jacket because it is so hot.

Yet, somehow, these kids have a joy that is indescribable. I have yet to meet one person, in any developed nation, as generous, loving, and happy as one of these children. This extreme contrast of having so little but loving so big makes me imagine what would happen, if I asked one of the children, "What do you do?" I don't think they would be so thrown by this question. They have less than most people I know. Their jobs are probably a lot harder, too. Yet, somehow, they don't allow this misappropriated value weigh them down.

Maybe instead of feeling ashamed of what you do, you speak it boldly, and keep your head held high because what you do isn't a reflection of your value.

Are you beginning to see how the Social Terrain puts undue pressure to do needless activities, none of which relates directly to your purpose?

Risk

We have more opportunity than Beethoven, more education on writing thank Shakespeare, more visual stimulus than Vincent Van Gogh or even Picasso who was alive in this past century; yet, everything seems riskier than ever before.

Risk deserves its place in this conversation. Risk is when you are deciding to take a bold step and are unsure of the effect. A major misconception about risk is that we can avoid risk with inaction.

Waiting or indecision could be just as risky—if not riskier—than acting. There is no way to avoid risk in life. That is impossible. Plus, considering the myriad of decisions one person makes every day, it is understandable why we want to avoid as much risk as possible. Too many decisions to make, and when it comes to the big ones, sometimes we are already exhausted.

2008 versus 2018

The Social Terrain also changes over time. Thus, the Social Terrain for young adults ten years ago was different than the Social Terrain young adults are facing today. It will change again in the future.

Today, the current Social Terrain must embrace lifelong education, multiple career paths, dense intellectual risk, and a whole new variety of social pressure from just ten years ago. How you navigate through this terrain makes all the difference.

As the Social Terrain advances, we have to look out for the changes and shifts in pressure we may face. We also have to analyze our decision making. In other words, sometimes we go toward a certain decision because we don't want to be like our parents. We pivot to do the opposite when the opposite may not be a good option either. For instance, not going to college because your parents went to college isn't a good reason. Being different for the sake of being different is not the point. The Social Terrain we were brought up in is important to identify so that we realize why we do what we do.

Thus, the better we understand its force on our life, the better prepared we are to overcome it.

Fear

Underneath the Social Terrain, there is one player. Fear.

Here is fear again, trying to make its place in your life.

Fears come in a myriad of forms and too often we give fear the position of deacon, right underneath the high priest, Jesus. We give Jesus his room and we give fear his room as well.

Aung San Suu Kyi, who led a nation through a twenty-five-year battle for democracy from repressive military rule, stated, "A most insidious form of fear is that which masquerades as common sense or even wisdom, condemning as foolish, reckless, insignificant or futile the small, daily acts of courage which help to preserve man's self-respect and inherent human dignity."

In fact, fear trickles into the belief that the only way to make a living is from a college education and a nine-to-five job. It trickles into accepting the status quo. It trickles down into being risk adverse and taking the path of least resistance. It trickles into people pleasing and giving up on our dreams.

When our decisions are heavily influenced by the Social Terrain and the Social Terrain is underpinned with fear as the common denominator, our most important task is to propel our purpose forward.

In The Middle

Imagine that you are sitting in the middle of the ocean. You left the dock four hours ago and are not set to arrive at your destination for another five hours.

When you are sitting in the middle of the ocean, with no land in sight, there are a lot of uncontrollable forces and factors. The wind pushes you. Waves bring you down. The sky can pour.

In the middle, it seems like things just happen to you.

As the term suggests, 'young adults' are in the middle. We are in the middle. We are young adults who are in the middle of life. We are young in the middle of school. We are young in the middle of our relationships. We know where we started. We know where were we want to go in some form or another. Yet, found in the middle, we have no idea how to make sense of all the external forces that shape our life. Education, relationships, debt, family, work, money, and the list goes on. Just being a young adult, in the middle, makes everything confusing.

Deep down, we feel a deep passion for our life and want to make sense of it.

But, when things don't go according to plan, in the middle, it seems everything is out of our control.

The Social Terrain will make it feel like you are being pressured by a lot of forces. When really, you have the power to shift those forces.

The Emergency Room

One time, I was waiting in an emergency room with my friend. His mother had just had surgery. It was late at night, and there were a lot of people inside the waiting room. Some were old and some were young. Everyone came from different backgrounds. It was in a low-income area. You can guess the atmosphere of the room. People were sick, hurt, and suffering. This left people tired, frustrated, and bored.

My friend went and asked people if they needed prayer. Most people denied him. Then, one lady who had originally refrained from receiving prayer came and asked him for prayer.

After my friend offered prayer to everyone in the waiting room, it was still a room of sick, hurt, and unhealthy patients. But now, the patients were interacting with God. You don't have to accept the social pressure, even if it is clearly defined. And maybe, just maybe, when you do act, people will transform.

Ice-Cream Living

Imagine a child walking up to the counter at an ice cream shop and ordering her favorite treat. She is given the option of ordering a one scoop cone. She loves both mint-n-chip and cookies-n-cream and decides to get one scoop of cookies-n-cream on a sugar cone. The person behind the counter whips up an overflowing cone and hands it straight to the child. With wide eyes the child grabs the ice cream, and right before the first lick, she looks around and does not see her father.

Her father will pay for the ice cream. Her father told her to go order the ice cream and that he will come and pay. But, as she keeps looking around, she doesn't see her father. The little girl had walked a few steps from the counter. She then returns to the counter to let the clerk know she won't be able to have the ice cream.

Then, as she hands it back to the clerk, the little girl turns around and heads back toward the carts to find her father. Her father sees her and asks how the ice-cream tasted.

She reclaims the entire story to him.

Then the father smiles, kneels down and tells his little girl with a calm and loving heart, "Honey, I already paid for the ice cream. I paid for it as soon as we walked into the store."

You already have freedom from the Social Terrain. Now, you must walk it out.

Believe in Me

Jesus made an unbeatable promise. It's pretty over-the-top, if you ask me. He gave us all authority (that He has in heaven), here on earth. Then he said this, which is just stupidly enormous.

"Truly, truly, I say to you, he who believes in Me, the works that I do, he will do also; and greater works than these he will do; because I go to the Father."

Yet, somehow, the pressure of the Social Terrain (our parents' suggestion to go to an expensive college, to take a job we dislike for a little more money, or when we do something out of the only idea of being different than the past), makes this statement empty.

It seems incomprehensible that we can do greater things than what Jesus did on earth. Nevertheless, he said it. The best thing we can do is believe.

Now that you know the Social Terrain of life exists, you can overcome it. You can choose to no longer be influenced by it and rather influence it.

People whose thinking is active in one direction, who employ everything as material, *who always zealously observe their own inner life and that of others*, who perceive everywhere models and incentives, who never tire of combining together the means available to them.

Friedrich Nietzsche,
a profound philosopher

Purpose Built Young

Your Dark Voice

What ought a man be?
Well, my short answer is 'Himself'

FROM *PEER GYNT* BY HENRIK IBSEN (1867)

Your dark voice will do everything it can to try and stop you from reaching your full potential. It is that loud amplified voice inside that rationalizes irrationally, hates effort, and takes everything personally.

In essence, your dark inner voice will always ask you the same exact question:

Do you have the courage to overcome me?

Your dark inner voice, as it may seem against you, is actually your best ally. It tells you exactly what you need to do.

Introduction

He who has a WHY to live for can bear almost any HOW.

FRIEDRICH NIETZSCHE, PHILOSOPHER

A contract is conditional. A job is conditional. A warranty is conditional. Value is conditional. Temperament is conditional. Even character is conditional. Most things in life are conditional—that if A happens, then B will happen; or if A happened, then B already happened. If I sign the contract, then the contractors will begin work. Or, I worked last week so I received a paycheck .

True love is unconditional. It means that it is given without any expectation in return. Well, so is your purpose. It is unconditional. It is 100 percent yours. It is guaranteed better than any warranty or contract.

Unconditional purpose is measured by the occurrence of human life, ignoring any advancement gained from someone's position, power, or possessions. It has nothing to do with talent or success.

Purpose is unconditional as it is in everyone. If it was in only a few, it would be conditional. It would mean that it was earned. And if it was earned, it wouldn't be in true love.

That means you're indispensable to His Great Plan. That means you are essential. That means what you decide to do matters. Our purpose statement is:

"Purpose is unconditional; your choice to fulfill it is optional."

Whether or not it was explained to you or people treat you as if it's not true, your life has purpose. It doesn't matter what your parents did (or didn't do). It doesn't matter if your parents call you an accident or if you feel you have no place in life. It doesn't matter what the world says to you. Today's fast-paced world doesn't change a thing. Purpose is unconditional. Your desire to grow, build, and become someone greater is a living testimony that your life has purpose.

Purpose

Overview

We needed to stop asking about the meaning of life, and instead to think of ourselves as those who were being questioned by life—daily and hourly. Our answer must consist, not in talk and meditation, but in right action and in right conduct. Life ultimately means taking the responsibility to find the right answer to its problems and to fulfill the tasks which it constantly sets for each individual.

VIKTOR FRANKL, SURVIVOR OF THE HOLOCAUST,
PRISONER OF WAR IN AUSCHWITZ

Imagine that you have just been given a task to create a toaster from scratch. Here's the catch: you need to source all your raw materials. No Amazon Prime or Internet bargains. You need to go and get it yourself. If you need some steel, you need to mine for it and get the iron from the rocks. No local hardware store or salvage yard.

Would you be able to do it? How many different pieces and places in the world would you have to travel to get every piece of plastic, metal, steal, and copper necessary for the toaster?

Thomas Thwaites, a young designer, recently set out to do this. He took everything out of the cheapest toaster he could find and disassembled it into an insignificant 400 separate parts! He would have to source and manufacturer each and every one of those pieces.

For example, he needed iron to create the steel grill and the springs. You cannot have a toaster without springs, so where do you source iron? Thwaites is from the UK and very little mining—if any—happens in the UK. He found one abandoned mine. After going to the mine, sourcing the material, going underground to get it, digging it up, he now had to extract the metal from the rock.

"My first attempt to extract metal," Thwaites related on The Toaster Project website (www.thetoasterproject.org), "involved a chimney pot, some hair-dryers, a leaf blower, and a methodology from the fifteenth century—this is about the level of technology we can manage when we're acting alone."

After all of Thwaites' genuine effort, the iron was still not pure enough to fit its purpose. The time required to develop this type of learning and trial and error was arduous.

Next, to create the electrical wires, Thwaites would need copper. Copper would form the prongs for the plug, the wire to send the current to the toaster, and the wires within the toaster to toast the bread. Copper would be able to transmit the electrical current through a plug and then into each and every tiny wire inside the toaster.

Purpose is much more a discovery process than a manufacturing process. The assembly line—to be molded, folded, boxed, and shipped—takes little appreciation for life.

To make a simple, less than $10 toaster, took Thwaites months. After traveling to various places, sourcing a few materials, and spending nine months on the project, Thomas only could get the toaster to work for exactly five seconds!

"And for about five seconds, the toaster toasted, but then, unfortunately, the element kind of melted itself. But I considered it a partial success, to be honest," Thwaites said in London in a 2010 TED talk1.

Our lives should not be satisfied with being a partial success.

It takes a lot more work and energy to try and manufacture something from scratch that has been designed, sourced, and already created. Purpose is the same way. We were created with a specific design. You have hundreds of components that build up to make you, you. Probably even skills and talents that you don't even know about.

Viktor Frankl came to a similar conclusion. He said, "It did not really matter what we expected from life, but rather what life expected from us."

This is essential to your life's work. What 'pulls' you up every morning? You have the power to cultivate a sense of purpose. Character cultivates a sense of purpose.

Purpose will give you an intense hunger for bringing to life what is already inside of you. That something that desires greatness. To be the best in the world. We have an immense power to help improve others' lives every day. Anything that holds us back from bringing out our best, we need to disregard. We have no need to manufacture our value. All we have to do is bring it out.

Just like a toaster, it's time to un-box the contents, plug it in, and find out its true value.

Scary, Big, Enormous

PURPOSE... is one of the simplest words, yet it can also be a scary, big, enormous word. The word seems to elicit so many emotions in people—often bad. The misconception that purpose is only some type of gifting for the elite and ultra-successful is a lie.

Discovering purpose can be derived from your relationships, your vocation and mastery. It is the ways you add value to your community.

Purpose, that scary, big, and enormous word, really isn't as intimidating as it seems.

Camo Jackets Are Fashionable...

If you want to fit in. Our purpose—our unique, person-specific purpose—is not for camo attire. What makes you different than 7 billion people on the planet? A lot of things.

It's like going through all the challenges of creating something as elegant as the iPhone, yet looking like a cheap flip phone. Why would you do that to yourself?

The Paradox of Purpose

"If you are living," A.W. Tozer wrote, "because it is the best alternative to dying, then, what good is it?"

We are completely able to be affected by our surroundings. We are vulnerable to what happens around us. At the same time, we still have a choice to create a future we desire. The tension is having courage in the midst of a world of unforeseeable outcomes. Anything good or bad could happen at any moment. Purpose doesn't only give you reason; it gives you direction.

The paradox of purpose is that you must be completely intentional while you are completely vulnerable at the same time.

Open the Box

We begin this section with the firm belief that whoever created the toaster had a design, sourced the right materials, and created the machine. In the same way, we toasters could end up in full use, serving warm bread or live in the box.

Most of the time, people never open the box. Because opening the box means they could fail. It means that they could stop working and need a fix. The toaster could look useless, meaningless, and worth nothing. We dump what is useless quick.

People refrain from following their purpose because of what it could potentially call from them. Or, that they can fail. Or that they could be so successful that they do things they never thought were possible.

That lifestyle is very unsatisfying. Just open the box.

Reason Everything Exists

When a human understands why they exist (and truly feels it in their heart), something magical happens.

Their energy wakes them up, feeds them, and keeps them up late. Their possibilities for the future help them perform at their peak every day. There is a reason everything exists and that means there is magic for everything.

Culture Asks

[The enemy of our soul] does everything within his extensive power to prevent us from discovering who and what we are.

A. W. TOZER, PASTOR, PREACHER, AND AUTHOR

Netflix Originals created a show based on the characters of Madagascar, the movie series. The show is called All Hail King Julien. The plot centers around an absent minded and hilarious King Julien who loves to dance and be king. He takes life at a very basic level. King Julien inherits the throne of the lemur kingdom and becomes 'Lord of the Lemur Kingdom,' at a very immature state of life (he loves dancing and dancing all night long... that is all). While the Kingdom is not defending itself from the Fossa, who come to attack the lemurs, King Julien 'helps' to advance the kingdom. One day, King Julian stumbles into a box of diapers. They are all lemurs and have no idea what a diaper is used for. Though, in that moment, the diaper becomes the most fashionable item in town. King Julien puts on a fashion show and soon every lemur needs one.

There was limited supply of the diapers, so the lemurs who didn't get one end up feeling as if they are missing something. They begin to sell everything they have to get one. They begin to cause divisions between the lemur Kingdom. These diapers begin to make everyone compare themselves to others.

This is the same thing we do with purpose. Some people feel purposeless. They feel purposeless because they look at others who appear to have a defined purpose. It's as if they are missing something. As if there is only a limited supply.

This is tied to our ideas around success and what we define as a successful life. It could be lots of followers, the right relationship, or fame. In any event, a majority of people walk around purposeless.

Ironically, it's easier to spend time finding success. Success is not hard to achieve, purpose is.

Just like the toaster example, you have to get plugged into the Creator to bring spiritual power to any thing you do. To bring purpose out, in a world of fashionable diapers, we need to know what we are spending our time plugged into.

Your Most Current Task

Your most current task is: Am I doing what I was designed to do? Can I love people more today? Can I serve people more today?

Don't let the world and the opinion of others shape your future.

We are more than a daily dose of caffeine, a few phone messages, or a weekend of late nights. We have things that will make this world a better place. Emailing ten people, texting five people, or checking twenty notifications is easy. Living a purposeful life takes much more intentionality.

No one will be able to bring it to life except you. No one will see it until you do. The question is, what is your most important task today?

What Do You Do?

Many will miss their life's dream because it is stored aside until after the rent is paid. We were taught to put our dreams on the backburner for 'someday' in the future. So, we wait. And in the meantime, more bills pile up: the car, the closet, the phone, and the cable TV provider. Not that any of those are bad. Rather, the contrary. They are just heavily sedating.

Making sure you are covered is important, but it isn't the thing we are called to do. The question becomes: how can I ever discover what God has placed in me if the majority of my focus is taken up with demands of what I can do for myself and my immediate needs?

Life's Primary Valuation

Life is not primarily a quest for pleasure, as Freud believed, or a quest for power, as Alfred Adler taught, but a quest for meaning. The greatest task for any individual is to find meaning in his or her life.
HAROLD S. KUSHNER, AUTHOR OF *WHEN BAD THINGS HAPPEN TO GOOD PEOPLE*

Sadly, meaning can never come from a bigger paycheck or a bigger house. The world may put high demands on us, but our goal to live with purpose is much bigger and more fulfilling.

Society wants to know if you have taken the road of success or the road of meaning. Others will want to box you in to a forum of their definition of success.

When I graduated from college, I couldn't find a job for four months. I was broken inside. I felt like a bipolar job seeker. One moment I was optimistic and another I was ready to give-up and live in a hut under the freeway. What I was realizing was that I was internally broken. When I finally did get a job, I still was internally broken. When I told people I found a job, they smiled and said "good." They never asked about me again.

Then, six months later, I was fired. After that, I went to work for another company doing a similar task, data entry. Why did I take another data entry job?

When I told certain people about it, they didn't even question it, they didn't even ask what the job was; they just said "take it."

People smile at a pay raise, new home, or bigger platform; yet, God,

He looks to your ability to promote the gifts He gave you.

It's more important for you to find freedom (in whatever life circumstances you find yourself in) than to make a lot of money, to have your doctorate, or get praise for things that are only material.

If you are completely broken inside, a new home, a new outfit, or new paycheck means nothing in terms of meaningful growth .

Viktor Frankl called it tragic optimism. Tragic optimism is finding the reason that you will turn pain and suffering into achievement and accomplishment. As every seed is birthed in a dirty place, your maturing (building character) can (and should) expand your purpose.

Challenger: Your Dark Voice

Our parents look at us…
'Child,' they say, 'You have all opportunity…
will you take it?'
'Yes, I must,' we say.
They say, 'Then go, my child…go.'

We are stuck ashore.
'Why?' they ask.
'Because I am still deciding…
I am still deciding.'"

DAVID ISKANDER (PARABLE OF THE PARADOX OF CHOICE)

The Faint Whisper of Light

In the presence of the dark inner voice comes something, all together, unique. It is the faint whisper of light. The voice that tells you, 'it's possible.'

The faint whisper of light is courageous. It is strong. It is of a quality that is pure and undefiled. It has integrity and backs its word. It makes your next level less of a challenge and more of an opportunity. The faint whisper of light says: despite a myriad of choices, high levels of responsibility, and an overpowering inner dark voice, this is a great day to be alive!

The faint whisper of light can call you into uncertainty, the unknown, and difficult situations. It will do it in such a way that makes you see beyond the immediate doubt and fear and realize a new level of courage and confidence.

Those who make intentional living look easy and can make decisions quickly have tackled an internal battle.

The faint whisper of light will give you clarity when it comes to your ability to push beyond the dark inner voice and believe in yourself. It will make your dilemmas of life (should I take this job or not, go to this school or not, move to this city or not, date this guy or not) no easier, but much more transparent on what you need to do.

The challenge is the faint whisper of light is faint. It is always there, yet faint. Thus, the better you can clearly hear the faint whisper of light, the more attuned you will be to its opportunity.

The Dark Voice

The dark inner voice is shrewd and cunning and will do everything in his power to keep you where you are. It will tell you to play the blame game. It will make you a victim of life. It will tell you to sit and wait until 'they' fix it. It will complain about the good in your life. When the dark inner voice wins, you are no longer held responsible. You give your responsibility to the world, and the world then decided what happened to you. It will tell you to not to believe. It will walk you toward doubt and fear.

Your dark inner voice will tell you not to try something because you are younger (or because, God forbid, you are older). Your dark inner voice will tell you: they have more experience; therefore, they know better. It will keep you from doing what needs to be done. It will keep you from being a leader. It will keep you from fighting for the first thing you should fight for—your purpose.

The dark inner voice will argue that 'this way' is the only way. It will confuse you. It will make you feel the fork in the road ahead is unmanageable. It will always bend toward what you know. The dark inner voice will even come from kind friends who suggest shying away from trying something new, big, or world-class. Your mind will run their doubts in your head as valid, fate, and non-negotiable.

One key trait of your dark voice is universal (everyone has it). It reacts to growth, building, and improvement the same way—it pulls out all the forces to stop it. It is present, appearing, and found everywhere and in everything you do. It's in your health, in your writing, your schooling, your relationships, and most definitely, in your purpose.

Sometimes, it comes in the form of a bad boss, teacher, or roommate. Or, in a close relationship like a girlfriend, mom, dad, or close friend. People who try and stop you from doing what you feel inside yourself is possible (reaching your full potential).

Another key trait is that the dark voice is persistent. It's right alongside every new venture, pushing for more headroom. Your greatest challenger to living a life of purpose is not some exterior posture, but an internal battle.

Your spirit has this constant beckoning to grow, build, and become greater. This always rubs your dark voice the wrong way.

The Challenge of Choice

In a TED talk titled The Paradox of Choice, Barry Shwartz makes the point clear and insightful[1].

When we make a choice, we have three reasons, Shwartz discusses, that make us end up less satisfied with the results, than if we didn't have so many options.

First, when you do pick one option, you can always imagine that you may have picked a better option. This causes you to regret the decision you made because you question the satisfaction level you could have achieved.

Secondly, the opportunity cost of making a choice escalates this feeling of potential dissatisfaction. Opportunity cost is the loss of potential gain from other alternatives when one choice is made. For instance, when I choose to spend four dollars on a cappuccino, I give-up any option of using that four dollars on anything else (like an In-N-Out burger, buying a few songs, or the like). When you have lots of alternatives, you compare your choice to all the other alternatives and figure out things you may be missing out on. Therefore, you are left feeling dissatisfied with the choice you did make. Opportunity cost, with many alternatives to consider, makes it seem that all the other options could have been more satisfying.

Thirdly, and most critical to our study of purpose, is what Shwartz calls escalation of expectations. He explained it with this story:

"I went to replace my jeans after years of wearing these old ones, and I said, 'I want a pair of jeans. Here's my size.' And the shopkeeper said, 'Do you want slim fit, easy fit, relaxed fit? You want button fly or zipper fly? You want stonewashed or acid-washed? Do you want them distressed? You want boot cut, tapered, blah, blah.' On and on he went. My jaw dropped. And after I recovered, I said, 'I want the kind that used to be the only kind.'"

When you have tons of options, your expectations increase. If you have so many variations, you should have one that you absolutely love. Yet, this escalation of expectation actually causes you to be less satisfied with your choice, if your choice has even one flaw in it. If the jeans seem not be stretchy enough, then maybe you picked the wrong pair. When in truth, the pair of jeans you have on today are probably one of the best pairs ever made.

When it comes to purpose, you have so many variations on how to live out your life. Thus, when you don't have absolute love for something, you begin to feel as if we have made a wrong decision. Even great decisions—that are founded in love and service—seem to feel unfulfilling because the alternatives (you could be studying for an exam, working on a project, or eating) are highly attractive. That means great results seem less great.

The fact that you make any choices at all that leave you even remotely happy is astonishing! Restaurants have hundreds meal options, and you can substitute the fries for salad (or the salad for coleslaw... or the coleslaw for fruit...maybe go with the fruit). Colleges have hundreds of degree options you can choose with many minors. Career options offer lots of options as well. The amount of choices we make for even a pair of jeans is through the roof.

When it comes to your life, the most important decision you have to make is finding and knowing you are fulfilling your God given destiny.

The conclusion, as Schwartz said it best, "You really want to get the decision right if it's for all eternity, right?"

The Art of Choice

If we have more freedom, we have more choice; fortune will come to those who grab ahold of the choices in front of them.

One tenet of modern society is human dignity (freedom of choice). When this used to once be a luxury, it is now normal. What has become normal is actually the thing that has come to make our every day lives seem so poor.

Every single decision in your life weighs on you with the full burden of responsibility. From choosing your clothing, to your cell phone plan, to the times you attend church, to the job you take, to the person you marry, to the city you live in, to the color pen you use for your notes, to the ink thickness. Oh and not to mention the choice of paper you use to write on.

Your responsibility and choices, now more than ever, carry much more weight. Our once so precious freedom is now paralyzing. You can marry someone from your city, or state, or country, or an entirely different country. You can have a job that is within walking distance, car distance, plane distance, or remote distance. You can have a virtual assistant in Taiwan help you with your homework assignments, a web programmer in the Philippines, and a nutritionist in New York. All these options are available to you.

Choice is enabling, but when it comes to the most important pieces of our life, can it become a weakness more than an empowerment? We have to make a choice with our future, our freedom, our time, our energy, and our potential. That is no ordinary call.

To steward your future, your freedom, your time, your energy, and your potential takes a lot of effort. In the middle of that, you have to choose what to eat three times a day. Our brains are not wired to make so many life changing decisions every single day.

Too many choices make any choice you decide on drawn out, more thought intensive, and often, less satisfying.

The myriad of choices we are given today, from the food we order to the careers we choose, ask us to be much more attuned to hear the faint whisper of light.

Busyness

Busyness is the opposite of purposed living.

Just because one is busy doesn't mean one is productive. It is the same for living with purpose. Make your life purposeful and you will have more free time. Be more passionate about the work you do do, and when you have a big season, you will be able to work hard because you know exactly why you are doing every single task.

Salmon swim thousands of miles (upstream) to birth their children in the same waters they were birthed. It's an amazing feat of nature. They obsess over achieving their goal. They must swim against the current, up ravines, through rocks and mud to get to where they started. If they swam upstream, then toward the left, then the right, well, they would never make any real progress. They would be really busy, but have little to show for it.

Rick Warren wrote, "You have just enough time to do God's will. If you can't get it all done, it means you're trying to do more than God intended for you to do."

Sometimes there are busy seasons. Rarely, should busyness be a lifestyle.

Busyness will make it hard to hear positive reinforcement from your faint whisper of light.

Death in Luxury

People have enough to live by but nothing to live for;
they have means but no meaning.
VIKTOR FRANKL

People die quicker from hopelessness than hunger.

Give a young man, who is weak and has not had a proper meal in eight days, a reason to believe there will be food tomorrow, and he can survive another day.

Hope is stronger than food. It's stronger than medicine. It's stronger than death.

On the flip side, if you are hopeless, you are dead. Many people die quicker from hopelessness than death. But, what happens to the time in between? From the point someone gives up hope to the point they actually physically die, they are lifeless.

Purpose gives you hope. Hope above your present circumstances, however bleak they may seem. Hope to overcome any of your struggles.

If purpose is unconditional, hopelessness will kill more vision, passion, and purpose today than at any time in history.

Me, Myself, and I

Emotional labor, in one view, is keeping certain feelings on the outside that may conflict with feelings on the inside. Emotional labor creates emotional disconnect and that leads to a lot of other negative emotions.

Emotional labor works in two ways.

Emotional labor comes in the form of continuing your work despite having a pain or problem. This is when someone is at work, at a job that treats them unfairly, and continues to come to work with a smile. It also comes in the form of pushing through the work to accomplish a desired outcome. This is when someone, despite people telling them it's not worth doing, continues to push through.

Both are examples of emotional dissonance. That is, when you experience a conflict between experienced emotions and your emotional actions. Emotional dissonance is healthy when it comes to pushing against the dark voice. It is unhealthy when it supports the dark voice. It is unhealthy when it counters your heart's highest desires.

When it comes to your life and your future—no one can tell you how to live. Only you can resolve this mental tension.

Many people are preoccupied with external struggles. What one must understand is that every external struggle is a reflection of an internal battle. We miss our inner state by being preoccupied with our external situations. We may not like our job. There may be issues with our friends. Whatever it is, we then turn to palliative solutions like drugs, alcohol, and entertainment to mask our inner state. When we separate our condition from ourselves, the tension doesn't go away no matter what we do.

This inner conflict takes energy and can leave us feeling broken, empty, and dry. Yet, emotional labor happens in either case (if we listen to the dark voice or not). Now, it's up to you to decide, which lifestyle will you choose?

Attitude

Attitude is a big indicator of who is winning that internal conversation. A positive attitude can be the attitude we choose, despite hardships, because our faint whisper of light has reminded us that God is in complete control.

How Does This Change Your Life?

In a last violent protest against the hopelessness of imminent death, I sensed my spirit piercing through the enveloping gloom. I felt it transcend that hopeless, meaningless world, and from somewhere I heard a victorious 'Yes' in answer to my question of existence of an ultimate purpose.
VIKTOR FRANKL, SURVIVOR OF THE HOLOCAUST, PRISONER OF WAR IN AUSCHWITZ

Say you have a dream to show tens of thousands of people the love of Jesus in a part of the world that is highly restricted against the Gospel with covert missionaries everywhere, equipping them, sending them out, and supporting them. Instead of waiting, you start (today) by meeting up with one person at a local school grounds to do a Bible study. (This is how I got saved.)

Say you want to be a world class photographer who uses their photos to create empathy and show people in developed nations the painful truth of war in war-torn countries. To start that journey, rather than just applying to big photo companies, non-profits, or waiting for a big paycheck to fund it all, what if you start (today) by taking photos of poverty in your city and sharing them. You will be surprised by how other people react to the poverty in their own city.

The Force is With You

There is no one way to do this. There is no one way to live purposefully. That would eliminate the identity and calling from your life. That would make you a boxed toaster, just like every other toaster that comes from across the ocean.

I made a small set of decisions that set me on a life of purposeful living:
1. Stop believing the hoax that tomorrow is a better day to start (Start today)
2. It's better to be fully committed and get it wrong, than sit on the fence for the rest of my life (Hustle)
3. I'd rather be broke and happy than rich and miserable
4. The force is with you (Believe in Yourself)

What purpose consists of is simple: internal freedom, person-specific goals, and out beating your current best. When it comes down to it, purposed lives pioneer.

Your life plan will alter. No worries. Explore. Enjoy it. Test things, and adjust when things are not working. It's a bit paradoxical, but we are able to handle that. On one hand, you need to make intentional decisions about where you are going, and on the other hand, you may change course very quickly.

Once you tap into it, you begin to overcome your current struggles. You have a force of nature pulling you up every morning. It's like a light. Your light, when set in a direction, has a determination to go in the route it is set to follow. You begin to focus on strengthening only those things which cannot be taken from you, that you know will be with you no matter what. It will pull you up every morning. In the bleakest situations, your force makes life full.

When you wake up a few hours early or stay up late to practice your craft despite having to go to a job you don't enjoy, you are grabbing it. When you invest in yourself by reading constantly, you are grabbing it. When you seek out mentors and friends who inspire you to become better, you are grabbing it. It doesn't really matter where you are today. What matters is the force within you.

Invisibility

If I was invisible, I would be released from so much fear and insecurity. The Social Terrain of modern culture would disappear. I would dance in the car, sing a lot louder, and take more risks. In essence, I would dance more often with my purest motivations.

With invisibility, I am less connected to people and situations that can hurt me. I am more available to put everything on the line to love and serve others.

This is the power of an amazing actor. Think of Benedict Cumberbatch, who plays Sherlock Holmes's in the modern BBC version. His actions are amazing. He plays Sherlock so well you almost forget that he is acting.

What if today, instead of being you, you were invisible (you played a role beyond iden-tification)? A heartfelt, strong woman with a high calling and purpose. Or, a man of strength and courage fighting for the freedom of others. What new qualities would you possess?

It makes sense for us to play our role because people are broken, they carry more baggage than they show, and truthfully, we need more daring people. What new quali-ties would you possess if you were invisible? What drawn-out fears would you confront?

This exercise may release you from yourself. It may actually make you invisible.

Choosing Right

In today's world, it is more possible than ever before to live a full live than in any other age of human history; it is just as possible to live an empty, void, semi, and spiritual bipolar existence.

They say that this generation will be the most lost, most confused, most off track. We will have the biggest challenges concerning cyber threat, medical advancements that prolong life artificially, and choices to make about living on Mars. We can choose anything we want.

What true potential actually arises in our current state of affairs is out of every-thing we could choose, we choose Jesus. We choose the One when there are 10,000 things beckoning for our attention, every day. We are loyal without even trying.

Are we distracted? Yes... of course! We are distracted by Jesus.

Start Toasting

Even when you can manufacture a perfectly good toaster, it still relies on the infrastructure of an electrical system to power up. In the same way, humans now come into the world as toasters, and when they connect to a wall plug (the Holy Spirit), something magical happens.

They begin to leave a mark.

Purpose is activating already existing capabilities and strengthens them through practice.

The toaster, wall plug, and bread are all already widely available. It's not an opportunity. It's our obligation. Start toasting.

Winning the Fight

How does living with purpose change your life?

When you travel a lot, you learn to carry less. When you learn to love a lot, you learn to no longer need to carry internal luggage and baggage that just weighs you down.

Your character is what produces the ability to shed that extra luggage. Just like taking a shower to clean yourself up from yesterday's dirt, building character takes yesterday's dirt, last week's sin, and your life's collection of baggage and doesn't let it determine your future.

Living with purpose changes your life because you stop looking at life with a world of bad stuff and see what is possible for you to chart—your unique, person-specific course. Your own pioneering journey.

You begin to realize the things that challenge you are actually good for you. They help you grow. They help you shed off extra weight.

Therefore, believers, be all the more diligent to make certain about His calling and choosing you [be sure that your behavior reflects and confirms your relationship with God]; for by doing these things [actively developing these virtues], you will never stumble [in your spiritual growth and will live a life that leads others away from sin].

2 Peter 1 · Amplified Bible (AMP)

The two most important days in your life are the day

you are born and the day you find out why.

Mark Twain

Intro to Go! Guides

Before we begin to use the Go! Guide, I want to mention that there is a thread in everything these guides are set up to do. Question everything. Even what seems normal. Question sleeping eight hours a night. Question why you need to have three meals a day. You may not change these habits. Rather, learn to own everything you do. Don't do things because that is what is 'normal.'

Also, take time on these questions. To define your life purpose takes time. We will shrink the pressure as much as we can. Yet, you have to forge your own path. That means that you have to look at your life, remove the clutter, and find a route worthy of your best effort. When I say 'clutter,' I mean allowing your purpose to be sidelined by an immediate challenge, such as: I need extra cash; must find a job. Often, our most urgent challenge calls our attention. But that is no way to live because there will always be something urgent pressing for your time and attention. You are bigger than your most immediate need.

How you walk through sets of challenges says a lot about if you have identified your purpose. Identifying purpose is identifying the why to your life. Therefore, it doesn't matter what happens or how things work out. All that matters is that you know why.

This is a very introspective question and makes you take responsibility for the way you feel. Your conditioning toward stressful times is what identifies how far you have come with Christ. It reveals the true freedom you possess inside. This is always confronted on a person-specific basis. Someone else's challenge is not your challenge. It may be easy for you and it may be hard for them, or the other way around, it doesn't matter. You must confront your challenges. (The best part of it all: when you do begin to do this, you gain an internal freedom in yourself that no one can take away and people will admire).

Finally, remember that we tend to overlook the simple for the spectacular. Don't overlook the power of today for some grand tomorrow. Don't overlook your success today—whether big or small—when you are in the moment of an average day. If you look beyond today for the success your life inherently possesses, the world will offer you everything as a solution and leave you questioning your own soul.

It's time to align your life to your hopes, dreams, thoughts, vision, and purpose.

Go! Guide

This section below is important. If you feel you are struggling to answer the sections below, please go to purposebuiltyoung.com/resources and download the free PDFs that follow alongside this Go! Guide.

...It is not freedom from conditions, but it is freedom to take a stand toward the conditions.

VIKTOR FRANKL, SURVIVOR OF THE HOLOCAUST, PRISONER OF WAR IN AUSCHWITZ

Clarify your purpose: Write your purpose statement (say, for the next five years) in one sentence. When you finish writing this you will be the only one who can answer this statement. If someone asked, who could do this, you would say 'I am the one.'

→ _____

Here are three additional options to help you answer the question:

1. What is your life about? What guides your life? What on earth are you fit to do? What makes you unique?
Remember, your purpose is unconditional. Let's start from that basic foundation. What initial thoughts come to you? Write them below.

→ _____

2. What makes you happy?

Do you want to be a designer, a photographer, or an artist? Do you want to build new solutions for high-pressure issues? Do you have an ability to bring people together, to be hospitable, to love unconditionally? Maybe you would like to be an advertising executive, digital marketer, or data storyteller who brings valuable insight to the marketplace. Or, you like to be a scientist, a mathematician, a teacher in an underdeveloped neighborhood. Go through your hobbies, passions, and identify your purpose.

→ _____

_____

_____

3. What would you continue to pursue unfazed if the world rejected, dissed, threw you out, and laughed at you? Would it be getting rejection letters from publishers, no one showing up to your meetings, people laughing at your photos?

Look at it another way: If you knew you wouldn't fail (you had enough time, money, courage, and talent), what would you do with your life?.

When people say you can never be good at that can you ignore them? Honestly, at times, the thing we are supposed to do is something we have never done. It is something we have yet to accomplish. It's not a talent we discovered at five years old and will do until we are ninety-five.

→ _____

_____

_____

The best part of it all is that when you identify your purpose, you will discover that, living it out is a great way to improve the world while simultaneously improving yourself. Make sure that you have written your purpose statement before you move on. It doesn't have to be perfect. It's just important to have a place to start.

Your purpose statement supports you to make practical guided decisions in your day-to-day. Does that new job opportunity align better with your purpose than your current job opportunity? Is $50,000 of debt a year worth your education?

Identifying your purpose will give you a measurable rate of return on your energy each day. If your main goal in life is to comfort people, you can ask yourself if you comforted one person. If it is helping others, you can ask yourself if you helped one person. You have a way to see if you are truly going where you want to go.

Note: This question could lead you to an answer that is something you currently are not part of now. It may be something that you have ignored or just recently discovered. In either case, that is okay. God can work with that.

Now it's time to get specific:

Define what your purpose is in work, school, your family, your relationships, your marriage, and your child's life.

You will discover that knowing where you want to go in the major pieces of life makes every day more fulfilling. It will inspire you to spend an extra hour doing homework when you are tired because you know you want to excel in your class. You will spend an extra hour, after a stressful day at work, to play with your child because you know that you want to make them a great leader. Often these specific purposes are seasonal and they possess a clarity to help you identify what is important and what is not.

I left a few blank for you to add in any special areas of your life.

Purpose in work: _____

Purpose in family: _____

Purpose in school (education): _____

Purpose in relationships: _____

Purpose in marriage: _____

Purpose in children's life: _____

Purpose in... _____ : _____

Purpose in... _____ : _____

Purpose in... _____ : _____

Purpose in... _____ : _____

Vision Statement

Describe what you want to achieve in the future.
Use numbers and time-bound limits here.

→ _____

_____

_____

Now, we will move forward by using our purpose and vision statement to clarify our goals. Once we do that, we can simply the process of living a life that is intentional and purposeful regardless of what our current responsibilities, obligations, and time-constraints.

So, friends, confirm God's invitation to you, his choice of you. Don't put it off; do it now. Do this, and you'll have your life on a firm footing, the streets paved and the way wide open into the eternal kingdom of our Master and Savior, Jesus Christ.

2 Peter 1
The Message (MSG)

"For I know the plans I have for you," says the Lord. "They are plans for good and not for disaster, to give you a future and a hope."

Jeremiah 29
New Living Translation (NLT)

A Rendition of the Firebird
The Russian Tale

In a Kingdom of great stature and integrity lived a King with a remarkable, lush garden. At the epicenter of the garden, between all the flowers and bushes, lay one rare tree.

Each day, this rare tree would bear one perfect apple. The perfect apple was the most exquisite and lovely fruit nature produced. This fruit, however, would puzzlingly disappear every night.

The king gathers his three children and proposes that they find the thief.

That night the two older children watch diligently, but as time passes, they see nothing and fall asleep. However, the youngest keeps alert all night. At the darkest hour, she sees a shining gold bird come and snatch the apple.

The young heroine swiftly chases this golden bird as it flew off! Unfortunately, she was only able to catch it by its feather. This left the young heroine unsure of herself. She felt unbecoming to let down the King.

One feather had fallen from this golden bird. The feather shone so bright that it lit up the entire palace. When the King awoke and saw the feather, he realized that his daughter had seen the mythical Firebird.

The Firebird had only been a tale of legend and a narrative of seeking life's highest attainment. The king then grieved over the Firebird and longed for the golden bird to be found. He proposed that whichever of his three children would find the golden Firebird would receive the kingdom.

On the search, the three siblings set out into the forest on three different journeys. One, not knowing where to go, quickly became idle. Another chose the first path available with little resistance. Then, the youngest sibling, chose the second path,
the path of highest resistance. It was marked as more dangerous to travel than the first path.

As each set-out, they were all tested with the same test. An animal came begging for food. The two older siblings fail this test by shooting at it. The young heroine willingly gives half of her food to the baby elephant. This was no ordinary elephant, however. This was the wisest elephant in the land. The young heroine's willingness to share allowed the wise elephant to become her guide.

The guide tells the young heroine the plan. She must go into a strange, foreign castle, alone. There, she is to capture the Firebird in the golden cage, not the wooden cage because the golden cage is the only one that can hold the Firebird. As the daughter goes into the cave alone, she panics and does the exact opposite of what she was instructed to do.

The king of the foreign castle then multiples the challenges in front of this young heroine. He instructs her to capture the Horse and the Golden Mane. In order to capture them, she must bring back the Golden Princess to the owner of the Horse and the Golden Mane. Every task presents a more challenging obstacle and tests everything this young heroine knows about herself.

To succeed in bringing about the Kingdom, she will be forced to mature and gain the confidence within herself to fulfill the call.

Determined to capture the Firebird, she treks deeper into the forest to capture the Horse and the Golden Mane. She approaches a second foreign castle, and this time, has an opportunity to regain her confidence. In her immaturity, the young heroine makes the same fatal mistake she made the first time.

The young heroine is slowly realizing that what is right in front of her keeps getting overlooked. That is, all the value she needs to capture the Firebird lies within her. The faint whisper of light beckons her to take courage. The golden cage is not something she will find in the castle, but something she will find in herself. It is an absolute quality that she must bring forth. At this point, she is fearful and anxious, but listens to the instructions of her guide.

To capture the Golden Princess, she must overcome this third test by doing exactly what the guide instructs. This time, she does.

She comes out with the Golden Princess by her side. She takes the Golden Princess to seize the Horse and the Golden Mane. Then, from there, she will take the Horse and the Golden Mane to retrieve the Firebird.

Now on her own, with no guide, she must take on every challenge to capture the ultimate prize worth all her effort, the Firebird.

Through the process, the young heroine slowly realizes that she is not acting solely in her interests. On the journey, she discovers that if she does not capture the Firebird, the grief of the King will spread to risk the safety of the entire community. She is herself fighting for a greater, selfless cause bigger than what originally compelled her.

To prove herself, she must rely on her inner qualities. Her call now, in climatic tension, is to finally capture the Firebird. As she gets knocked down time and time again, she makes the single resolution of always getting back up.

Then and there, in a different, obscure, darker, and even a more foreign castle, she finds the Firebird. She releases her capture of the Horse and the Golden Mane to capture the Firebird. This young heroine has now developed the golden cage she needs to capture the Firebird.

She immediately sets off for her father's kingdom to complete her quest as the true heir. When she arrives, her father, the King, bestows upon her the power and authority of the entire kingdom.

The young heroine can now rule with soundness, maturity, and proper objective judgment. She has uncovered the qualities within herself to take on such great feats. She now realizes that all the while she was thoughtfully chasing the Firebird, the Firebird was calling her.

The Firebird holds the gold that could light the room when you enter and advance the Kingdom. Those who do not choose to chase the Firebird, choose an empty life. Today we call this a reactionary lifestyle; it is dictated by the whims and flows of daily commissary life. This way of life is made to follow and never to lead. This life gives very little return on investment and makes a slave of man.

However, those who do answer the call risk hunger, frigid air, and even death. Those who do develop the golden cage and gain the character necessary to capture the Firebird in the most obscure and most challenging spaces realize their full potential. The Firebird unlocks the gold within them. The security that is built on position, power, or possession will not maintain the Firebird. The only cage that can hold the Firebird must be of supreme quality able to withstand time, unforeseen threats, and suffering.

The Firebird is a story about purpose. A story about the purpose you must set out to catch. A story about listening to the call despite setbacks, challenges, weaknesses, insecurity, fear, and doubt.

And that my friends, is **purpose built young.**

The Firebird is originally a folk-tale that takes on various Eastern European versions. The story I referenced was the Czech version.

2

Your Character

Your Character

When you want to increase the light in a room, you increase the kind of bulb itself. A bulb can only shine brighter if it has the inner caliber to withstand such high voltages. Or, it will just blow out.

To increase the light in our life, our internal caliber to withstand the storms of life must increase.

The biggest challenge for many is following with firm ability their strong moral compass. In the face of failure, discouragement, emotional labor, and the easily-sedating Social Terrain, one must be able to follow conviction. To do this, we will use the power of the Suitcase Characteristics.

The compilation of Part II takes a fresh look on living with character in a modern society that works day and night to minimize your inner strength.

Life Constriction 2: Setbacks

**You will find trouble in the world—
but, never lose heart, I have conquered the world!**

JESUS, JOHN 16

When you graduated college, you were ready to give yourself to a full-time corporate career just to realize that the company you desire, won't hire you. When your big dreams intersect a harsh reality, the pressure of finances and family expectations put you in a place of mental instability. You felt God on your entire journey through college. Now, the 'God of everything' is around you, but you do not feel Him with you. Your life dangling by moments of just hanging in there. You think, could I ever be a designer, a business leader, a minister? Will I impact anyone? Am I capable of more? Will I be bigger than this moment now? You are forced to make a job decision based on your most pressing need, a financial lack, rather than your highest calling.

You may feel like a talented designer who finds it comfortable working for a money-hungry firm that undermines talent and values for profit and new accounts. Or, you may feel like the person who knows they will run their own business yet settle working for a company that doesn't even pay enough to get by. It's not that these realities won't happen. It's that we allow these setbacks to determine our hopes, dreams, and goals for the future.

When we have the option to overcome the Social Terrain and fight for our purpose, our next constriction will be setbacks.

Setbacks

A setback, in a broad sense, is anything that gets in the way of achieving your goal.

Many setbacks are external cues (problems, changes, losses). These things can push us back from the goal we are trying to accomplish.

Conversely, the devastating setbacks are always internal. Our weakness, our failures, and our past. How could a lack of skill, a failed relationship, or a bad experience with our past keep us from our purpose? By the very nature of self-doubt. Setbacks have the power to speak louder in our minds than God's affirmation. These setbacks have a way of voiding any credibility in achieving our call. They make us feel inferior, useless, or unprepared.

Your character is the surest way to battle setbacks. It will directly confront any fear, lack of hope, or past pain you may face. When you willfully get back up to try again, you undermine any power that setbacks will have on your life. Ultimately, you transform your future.

Your Game of Tennis

Each setback carries one major caveat.

Every setback has the power to throw you off course: to undermine the course God has opened up for your life with opportunity, resources, and relationships around you. At the same time, every setback has the power to propel you - in an exceptional way - further down the right course.

Just like a game of tennis, as the opponent hits the ball across the court to you (a setback), you prepare to hit the ball back across the court towards the opponent in aims to win. Your sole intent is winning. And to win you must do better than every setback that gets hit toward you.

There are people in the game, and there are people who sit on the sidelines and watch the game. You are in the game. You wouldn't be going to church next weekend if you were out of the game. You wouldn't be studying the scripture if you gave up on the match. You wouldn't be working the job you dislike to pay off school debt. You wouldn't be reading this book if you weren't still in the game.

Now, it's your turn.
You're up.

Suffering

But there was no need to be ashamed of tears, for tears bore witness that a man had the greatest of courage, the courage to suffer.

VIKTOR E. FRANKL, *MAN'S SEARCH FOR MEANING*

My friend, Kenric Tran, called me to go with him to visit his mother in the hospital. We had just come back from a mission trip together about a month before. His mother's condition was getting worse. She had just been admitted to the intensive care unit. Her kidneys were failing. She would awake time and again, and her dementia was causing her to wake-up unaware of where she was and why she was there. Surrounded by beeping machines, tubes running in and out of her, and an intense hospital scene, Kenric was the key decision maker for his mother's deteriorating health. He was only 26-years-old.

That day at the hospital, we prayed for his mom. In the middle of all this, Kenric was forced to deal with the unresolved tension that his mother, who may lose her life at any moment, does not know Jesus. She did not even want to learn about Jesus.

Somehow, after visiting the hospital, that same night Kenric was praying for another young man. Gary was homeless and just 25-years-old. Kenric prayed for Gary, offered to purchase him food, and didn't even tell Gary about his own struggle.

How do you have the courage to walk gracefully through suffering?

Elisabeth Elliot in A Path through Suffering defines suffering as having what you don't want or wanting what you don't have. Suffering in the form of grief, distress, pain, or sorrow may be the single greatest challenge for believers. Suffering challenges everything we believe, where we find our security, and our belief in God.

Most of us were never taught how to deal with suffering. It wasn't taught in high school after math class or talked about in the job description.

Introduction

Our lives can only exalt one.

JD GREER, PASTOR

Humility is not the sidekick—humility is the superhero.

It is easier to have a big ministry than it is to have a big impact. To put it differently, one can be externally focused much more readily than internally positioned.

Humility is not the sidekick to your life story you pick up when you need it and leave it when you want; it is the **superhero**. And true humility only comes from Jesus.

Overview

The trouble with you and me and the rest of humanity is not that we lack self-confidence (as we're told by the world) but that we have far too much self-importance.

ANONYMOUS, *EMBRACING OBSCURITY: BECOMING NOTHING IN LIGHT OF GOD'S EVERYTHING*

Sunday, July 6, 1924 was approaching fast. The Olympics were to be held in Paris. This was the second time Paris had hosted the international, multi-sport event. Over 3,000 Olympiads trained, prepared, and made the arduous journey to Paris to represent their countries. On that day, Eric Liddell, an outstanding runner, would compete to race his best event.

Eric Liddell, Scotland's pride and joy, was set out to win the 100M. This was his best event. They called him the Flying Scotsman. As he competed for Great Britain, Scotland would take great honor in this remarkable feat since this would be Scotland's first gold medal. But he didn't do just that. Eric Liddell withdrew from competing in the 100m event.

He skipped the race.

His decision to skip the race was known well in advance. When Eric had looked at the schedule for the 100m race during the 1924 Olympics in Paris, nearly a year earlier, he realized he could not run it. Something within the Flying Scotsman, he would later be unapologetic about, convinced him not run the race.

It was not the an injury, Parisians, or his competitors. It was the date itself, July 6, 1924. July 6, 1924, the day of his best event, fell on a Sunday.

The British Olympic Committee was astonished at his decision. Many looked to Eric's decision as selfish. Others derailed his decision as immature. He was seen as a fanatic, overly religious, stubborn person. Eric stood firm by his answer, as Eric Metaxas recounts, "Sunday is the Lord's Day—not a day for playing games—even the Olympic Games. Instead, it was a day for rest and worship."

Some tried to convince him that he could do both—go to church earlier and race at the scheduled time. Eric didn't budge. When that did not work, his sponsors went to the International Olympic Committee and asked them to change the date of the race.

They had no luck there, either.

Eric's only option was to race in the 200m and 400m race. Both of which were not his best events.

"Liddell was a world-class sprinter, not a world-class quarter-miler." A 100m race is built around sprinters that depends on speed. A 400m race is built around a runner who depends on stamina. The endurance levels are entirely distinct.

This story is a measure of a man's character—to reveal what a man will stand for relentlessly. It was what God looks for as He searches the earth. Those who come with the right heart. A heart that will submit in times of pressure.

Dictionary Definition

The modern dictionary definition of humility states (adjective)[1]:
1. not proud or arrogant; modest
2. having a feeling of insignificance, inferiority, subservience, etc.
3. low in rank, importance, status, quality, etc.; lowly
4. low in height, level, etc.; small in size

This definition draws a lot of feelings but mainly one. A sense of unimportance. The reason I began my study on humility was because it was so evidently important to our walk, but I barely understood it. I soon realized that the dictionary definition overlooks the main ingredient of being truly humble.

A succinct and detailed definition for Humility is understanding your place with God. Just like a seed that is properly planted in the right environment, at the right depth, in the right conditions, you will flourish most when you understand your place with God. Call it a clear path to eudaimonia. Conversely, think of a seed that misjudges its proper position with God. If you are too deep (too low), you will miss the potential value you get from the sun in your life. If you are too high, you will miss the potential value you receive from being firmly grounded with solid roots.

Best in the World

Seth Godin and Jim Collins do a fabulous job in their writing to depict the reasoning of why you should be best in the world at something[2]. The question for us then becomes: can you be the best in the world and be humble? Can you have a meek spirit with world-class quality?

I think we can quickly resort to an answer on the side of yes, it is possible.

And you would be right. Humility does not inherently come into conflict with one's life.

For example, imagine walking through one of Picasso's museum in Barcelona or Paris and finding out that the painting you are looking at is worth millions of dollars. Then, you are transported into time, into a small shopfront with various kinds of paint. Like a fly on the wall, you see Picasso come in to purchase the paint he will use for that same painting. It cost him less than $1.

The value of the painting isn't in the paint or the canvas. The painter's personality is what matters most. And for you, it's not necessary what you do or where you do it.

It's God's work that matters most. It's not the craft or the individual. Humility does not inherently conflict with one's work. Humility isn't subject to a strict line of vocations. It is not about the colors or the design as much as it is about the painter (God).

Your value, as the author of *Embracing Insecurity*, put it, "is not contingent on what you do or accomplish but entirely dependent on what He has done in creating you, redeeming you, calling you, and leading you."

That means, yes, you can be best in the world and be humble.

Humility is in having an internal position that is allowing God to lead the show while you play the role you are set out to play. Often, that means you will be highly exceptional and valuable. Your life is configured to be best in the world at something. Our mission is to bring this gift to life. And that duty comes with a responsibility: humility.

The Height of Grace

There is something profound and beautiful about humility that is paradoxical in every sense.

The height of grace in us is rooted in the depth of our humility. This happens in a particular fashion that is comparable to a Redwood tree. Redwoods can grow to hundreds of feet tall. Their roots, in turn, would assume to need to grow very deep to hold up against the weight of the tree.

However, the Redwood's roots normally only grow about five or six feet deep. But they extend out to the sides and interlock with all the other Redwoods around them. What a perfect depiction of humility. Humility is not undervaluing yourself. It's understanding your place with God and stretching your roots far and wide so that when the winds of life come and blow, the height of grace in you holds fast. Humility is depending on God. It is also depending on others.

If you don't imagine that the entire universe is at this understanding with God, then look again at the precision of the sunrise, the glow of the stars, and the wind that blows up and against your body, sending a chill down your spine. And what about how the powers of the clouds, winds, and waves commit to their lane. Understand your place before God and you unlock the freedom to live in your lane, content, with peace, and in full assurance that the God of everything is in control of all things.

When you take active steps to humble yourself before God, and make Jesus the leading role in your life, you begin to understand your place with God. You make Him superhero, not the sidekick. He will use you and move you and shake you and challenge you, and he will do all this to fill you with Himself.

Your inward stance toward an external circumstance is the gauge we measure by. If someone quickly upsets you when they mistreat you, maybe you can find room to humble yourself a bit more. Who cares if they are right or wrong? What matters is your choice to respond, to keep your peace, and your availability for God to moving in and through you.

Realizing Your Place

When everything is said and done, God does not need any new medals or honors of what he can garner for himself. What he longs for is us.

When Eric Liddell worked so hard, he trained, he stayed committed, he got early and made sure to give all the glory to God along the way, he was further challenged to give up what he deserved for what he knew was true. He could have said, 'I will make this one exception,' 'My family will understand,' 'I mean, God will understand,' or 'This opportunity is once in a lifetime, it would be my first gold medal, I have no other option but to race.' He did not use any of this reasoning. He stuck to what he knew to be true.

Eric Liddell could have brilliantly given the most intelligent reason to compete on the Lord's Day of rest—he worked so hard and gave so much, he got up early and disciplined himself, or that he had dedicated years of training for this moment. His entire country was rooting for him. But, he kept it simple because he had realized one truth. He had some overwhelming sense that everything was going to work out.

It seems he understood his place before God and that made him realize this essential truth of humility: you can take what you don't deserve, gracefully.

The principle of first shall be last doesn't only mean that if you start last, you will get to be first eventually. It also means you may be ahead and need to go to a place behind. Those who serve most gracefully are usually not searching for accolades or respect or awaiting it. Rather, they have their eyes on the expansion of the Kingdom. Just like Eric Liddell, one can get out of the way for God to do what He desires on Earth.

That is radical love and service.

Ziploc or Glad

Our lives are full of what we choose. Most of our lives we unconsciously throw things in—relationships, money, opportunities, hang-ups, experiences, dreams, desires, and the like.

Have you ever had some leftover food that you needed to put in a Tupperware container and you were stuck trying to choose the right size container?

You try and gauge the right size to hold all of the leftovers. When you find the right size, you grab it and begin pouring all the food into the container only to realize that it is just a fraction overfilled. There are two things you can do. One, you can grab a second container and throw the leftovers that brim over the top, into it. Or, you can do what I would do, you can try and stuff it all in.

This is what many will do with God. We often try filling our lives with so much that we long for—our dreams, our desires, our comforts—just to realize that we don't have enough God and give him a little room up top, where he barely fits.

He wants all of you. He wants you to understand that he always has your best interest at heart—the very core of Him. Don't give him the remaining brim to change your life. Empty yourself of your rights and obligations and comforts. Give him, you.

Don't be a container that is just overfilled and leave God little to no room to come in. Don't stuff God in at the very end. The chief cloak of grace and holiness in your life is a humble spirit. Have you ever had a friend who has an obvious problem, but they don't allow you to speak into their life? They know everything they need to know, are always right, and don't give you room to build them up. They have an excuse for every mishap and a reason for every failure. That is what happens when one does not have a humble spirit. God can never guide our course. If the Holy Spirit is the Spirit of truth (and hearing the truth is a struggle), if we only give God the brim of our Glad Tupperware containers, we leave little room for growth.

Race Day

On race day Eric Liddell set out to do his best. He was given the worst position on the track, the outermost ring. During a race, the person on the outer ring is unable to see where they compete with other athletes. It makes it difficult to gauge success.

Watching footage from the 1924 Olympics, you see a confident, young Liddell with his hands on his hips, and his head held high. As they prepared for the race, the gun went off. Liddell took off. He took the first turn with all enthusiasm and excitement. Then around to the next corner. He was in the lead. A few runners were jetting along and gaining speed, but Liddell kept his position for the entire race.

On Thursday, July 10, 1924, Eric not only won the 400m race, but he also broke the world record at 47.6 seconds for the 400m. His world record would not be beaten for another twelve years at the Berlin Olympic Games of 1936.

Compare Liddell's decision not to race on Sunday—despite all his hard work, early mornings, and grueling training—to Jesus who gave up unlimited peace, to be mocked and mistreated by people full of pride and fear, to clean the disciples feet, and to be beaten (none of which he deserved). Humility is no longer the sidekick to help us get through tough seasons. It is the main course. Humility is the superhero who saves the day.

Eric Liddell dealt with giving up his opportune moment to win a gold medal, something he had trained years to accomplish, to follow God's command. Let's rephrase that. Eric Liddell gained a new level of grace to win a gold medal, in a sport that was not his best that he had only trained temporarily for, to honor God's command.

Culture Asks

Humility before God is nothing if not proved in humility before men

ANDREW MURRAY, AUTHOR OF HUMILITY: THE BEAUTY OF HOLINESS

Amazing, Remarkable, Talked About

Seth Godin, a prolific author, speaker, and blogger knows how to add the value of being remarkable. In a 2003 TED talk based on his book Purple Cow, he demonstrates what gets noticed when people have millions of decisions to make and many things asking for their attention1.

During his talk he tells this story:

"And my parable here is you're driving down the road, and you see a cow, and you keep driving because you've seen cows before. Cows are invisible. Cows are boring. Who's going to stop and pull over and say— 'Oh, look, a cow.' Nobody.

But if the cow was purple—isn't that a great special effect?

If the cow was purple, you'd notice it for a while. I mean, if all cows were purple you'd get bored with those, too. The thing that's going to decide what gets talked about, what gets done, what gets changed, what gets purchased, what gets built, is: 'Is it remarkable?' And 'remarkable' is a cool word because we think it just means 'neat,' but it also means 'worth making a remark about.'

Our mind is tailored to block out the majority of things we see. Otherwise, we would be overloaded. People then naturally look for things that are amazing, remarkable, and worth talking about.

But, don't be a purple cow just to be different. That would not work. To be amazing, remarkable, and worth talking about, everything you must muster up to do is... be yourself.

Weirdness

Being a purple cow naturally creates a taste of weirdness to your walk as a Christ-follower. The world lives by an entirely different set of values.

This weirdness to our walk looks like a person fasting in the middle of the work week, an individual giving their tithe to the church, a person denying themselves and serving others. It looks like someone who leaves the comforts of their home and security to live in a developing nation. It's my friend praying for a homeless person. Purple cows are everywhere, we see them, we talk about them, and we tell their stories.

Jesus was a purple cow.

Eric Liddell was a purple cow.

You can become a purple cow.

But purple cows operate best in one zone. The zone of humility.

That means the more you align yourself in the zone of humility, the more purple you will become.

When you want to retaliate against the boyfriend who dumps you unexpectedly, you give it to God, pray, and move forward freely. When you lose a job, you know God is your provider. When you feel a whisper on your heart to pray for someone, you do. Your purpleness is just your natural Kingdom identity.

And what we identify with will bring forth how we can be purpler (or, in other words, our true selves).

Major Contrast

When you go outside the safety of your family, home, and relationships and come across all sorts of situations and challenges, you are either a white cow or purple cow. A light or not.

To grow and establish an entirely new secure base on heaven, let's look at the major contrast of the Kingdom against the success of the world set to the tone of the 3P's:

Position: The world asks you to be something or be someone.

Power: The world asks you to leverage something or own someone.

Possessions: The world asks you to have something or outrank someone.

Compare the 3P's against humility. Humility asks you to define yourself by who you are from within. Humility asks your ego to disappear so God can play the leading role in your life. The sure presence of God is in the disappearance of self. That's what our time on earth is truly asking us.

Humility gave Jesus position (with God), power (from God), and possessions (for God) during a culture that would regard him as small, ineffective, and meager. Somehow, the effect lasted for centuries. He was a light. In all reverence to our King, He was a purple cow.

You Are a Light

You are a purple cow. You are a light.

When you realize that you have X hours left to live, what would you do differently? Serve others, go on missions, not care about others' opinions, step out of your comfort zone more, or something else? What would it be?

This type of humility in culture makes you a purple cow. You are generous with who you are, what you do, and what you have. That is the exact opposite of what the world asks for. You stop exalting yourself and downplaying others. There are some not-so-smart cows out there, but that is okay. Invest more into them.

Humility is taking your place backstage to watch the show as Jesus takes his place front and center. What this does to you is beyond measure because you begin to understand your place in the grand scheme of things. You get to leave the theater, go back to your home, to a lousy job, to an unclear teacher, and simply smile because you were made to be a light in dark, dark, dark places.

Challenger: Suffering

Was mich nicht umbringt, macht mich stärker.
(What does not kill me makes me stronger)

FRIEDRICH NIETZSCHE, A PROFOUND SCHOLAR

Fight for Freedom

In 1990, Aung Sang Suu Kyi, the opposition party leader of Myanmar's first Demo-cratic Party was up for election. Myanmar is a country in Southeast Asia that had been ruled up until this time by oppressive military rule. She had rallied around the mili-tary-ruled country campaigning charismatically. Her message to the 40 million people of Myanmar: freedom.

With her clarity in speech and strong poise, she was the frontrunner for the first democracy in Myanmar for the benefit of the people. She talked about the hope that would bring together neighborhoods, towns, and the entire nation. She spoke of the hope it would bring for future generations.

"She united deep commitment and tenacity with a vision in which the end and the means form a single unit. Its most important elements are: democracy, respect for human rights, reconciliation between groups, non-violence, and personal and col-lective discipline." –Professor Francis Sejersted, Chairman of the Norwegian Nobel Committee, who awarded Aung Sang Suu Kyi the Nobel Prize for Peace in 1991.

Aung Sang Suu Kyi made it a striking point to continually outline the reason for a government that represented the people. "The people of Burma," she wrote, "view democracy not merely as a form of government but as an integrated social and ideo-logical system based on respect for the individual...They want the basic human rights which would guarantee a tranquil, dignified existence free from want and fear."

In 1991, she won the election by a landslide. The military rule received 21.2 per-cent of the votes. Aung San Suu Kyi's party, on the other hand, received 58.7 percent of the votes. This gave the party 392 seats out of 492 seats in government. A confident progress to begin the trek toward freedom for the people.

However, the military power negated the results, refused to give up power, and used strict force to stop the move toward democracy.

> The elections of 1990 are an important landmark in the modern history of Burma. After three decades… almost 30 years…of military dictatorship, finally the people of Burma were going to be able to vote for a government of their choice. The elections of 1990 were free and fair. It was one of the freest and fairest that had taken place in this region at that time. But unfortunately, the results of the elections were not honored.
> AUNG SAN SUU KYI, TEN YEARS AFTER THE 1990 ELECTION

Aung San Suu Kyi was placed under house arrest the same month she won the election. Her husband and children were exiled from Myanmar. Her colleagues were thrown in prison. There they were mistreated, beaten, and tortured. Aung San Suu Kyi and her party had worked so tirelessly and diligently for this election just for it all to be taken away from an overpowering military rule. She was to spend the majority of the next twenty years, up until 2010, under house arrest. She was limited with little access to see or talk to her family, and all hope for future freedom was taken away.

Sometimes our suffering comes as a surprise, like the results of the election. Or, as a slow creep in. It can be sudden, unexpected, or widespread. It can begin creeping unnoticed or hidden from our awareness. Then, it hits like a fast-moving train or a slow, arduous death.

What gave Aung San Suu Kyi the courage to fight for her country? Well, it was no one other than her father, Aung San. Aung San was the first general in Myanmar to fight for the freedom of the people. He was a leader in organizing the country's sovereignty from foreign rule. When he spoke about freedom, he made it clear:

"If we should fail to do this, our people are bound to suffer."

Our ability to deal with suffering, as we will see, is very close to our ability to bring about true change and freedom. To the surprise of many, twenty-five years later, Aung San Suu Kyi was back up for election, and again her party won. Today, her party is taking active steps to move the country of Myanmar toward freedom.

Futility in Our Suffering

It seems futile to call losing a job, a relationship, or feeling purposeless in life suffering.

I mean, aren't civil wars, death, and tragic natural disasters actual suffering? In comparison, feeling purposeless just seems so tiny and futile to call suffering. It seems pointless.

If that is true, these things would not then make us feel unworthy. It's hard to minimize a person's significance, and much more difficult, to minimize the pressure we find in our daily challenges. That is to say, none of our sufferings are futile because suffering is both physical and emotional. Remember our chat about emotional labor?

Feeling directionless can lead to waking up uninspired, being emotionally disconnected from life, and feeling run down by the world's constant advice for our situation.

People fail us, our parents fail us, we fail ourselves, and somehow our suffering is still just as real as death. Our internal suffering is just as real as our external suffering.

Suffering

Your dream job sends you the reply, "Thank you for applying.... Unfortunately..."

Your bills are piling up.

Your mother just found out she has cancer.

You are taking care of your parents.

You cannot get into the college of your dreams.

Your friends seem to all be doing better than you.

You aren't reaching your potential.

You feel run by fear.

You just wish you had a car to get to school.

You wish your parents would be more understanding.

You wish your body didn't have the illness.

You wish you were skinnier.

You are stuck working a job you actively dislike.

Suffering is ubiquitous. It isn't associated with one thing or problem. It can be found in every aspect of our life. This challenger poses the biggest threat to our humility. When we suffer, we struggle. And when we struggle we are faced with trying to see through cloudy waters.

Wanting what you don't have or having what you don't want are two very connected worlds. They simulate the mental agony that comes from life. They bring forth the suffering that comes in life.

What We Truly Deserve

Our spirits long for perfection. We were made perfect in His image. Inevitably, you will always get less than what you deserve. The challenge is finding humility in the middle of getting what you don't deserve. When we deal with many aspects of suffering, the statements starts with 'I deserve...'

When you feel you are suffering, what is it that is suffering?

Often, our ego. But, when you can freely allow suffering to take on its proper course, address it, and give up your rights, you gain ultimate freedom.

You can be offended, rejected, ridiculed, mistreated, spoken down to, disrespected and keep your peace. Life will always fall short. It all depends on what you expect you deserve, in a fallen short world.

When you shift focus from what you do to who you are, the question becomes less about what you deserve and more about who the world deserves you to become. Humility understands this well. Humility understands one's place with God. This allows you to give more than you deserve because He gave you more than you deserve.

Giving

Those who suffer the most have the most to give. The clearest form of love, the highest level of grace can come from your fellow man or sister who suffered much. It reflects freedom. It reflects Jesus.

A humble heart (one that can trust and get less than it deserves) can walk through difficulty at a much more peaceful pace. You need something that works again and again against this challenger.

That is, a humble, meek spirit that is positioned right with God gives most generously, wholeheartedly, and selflessly.

In an interview with Aung San Suu Kyi by Al Jazeera, conducted after her nearly twenty years of house arrest, the interviewer asked her about her struggles.

She was barred from seeing her family and her late husband, Michael, who passed away in the UK during her incarceration. She was the winner of the 1991 Nobel Peace Prize and gave her speech in 2011, twenty years later, after finally being released from house arrest.

"Frankly, I find it quite embarrassing when people ask me about my struggles and my sacrifices..." the Nobel Laureate answered. "My colleagues made many more sacrifices because they did not have the protection of the name that I had."

What Aung San Suu Kyi is referring to is that her father's name protected her. Her father was the pioneer of charting a course for freedom in Myanmar. People revered him.

This gave her the ability to give of herself generously, wholeheartedly, and selflessly.

How much does God's name protect us? How much more does all our suffering shrink in the eyes of our Suffering King who gave up his throne and then his life for us?

He was offended, rejected, ridiculed, mistreated, spoken down to, disrespected and kept his peace. He gave up the most and now we are given the most because of Him.

How Does This Change Your Life?

Is this the condition that I feared?
If you would not have a man flinch when the crisis comes,
train him before the crisis comes....
It doesn't matter how great is the flame,
but what it falls upon.

LUCIUS ANNAEUS SENECA, ROMAN PHILOSOPHER

The Elementary School Janitor

Steven was a 47-year-old elementary school custodian. He was married with one child.

On the last day of school, all the students were signing yearbooks. When the principle came out, there were a few students who came and asked for his signature in their yearbook.

Then, when Steven came out, the majority of the students ran to him and asked him to sign their yearbook. The custodian had a line of students waiting for him.

Humility is less about influence and more about impact.

A custodian can have more impact on his team than a principle, CEO, or any other high-level position. That is, the position doesn't automatically mean the person will impact people in a positive way.

Only you determine your impact.

"What's Next?" Mentality

A dear friend of mine (we will call him Tom) recently got engaged.

When we had lunch the other day he told me about the responses he has been getting from family and friends.

His parents were upset that he made such a big decision. He spoke with them beforehand, but they thought he wasn't financially fit to get married.

"Can you afford getting married?"

His friends were excited. They asked him, "When is the wedding?" Then, they asked him, "Where is the honeymoon?"

Tom had just made an incredible and important decision for his future, and the only thing people could speak about was 'what was next.'

When he started the relationship, people would always ask the question, "When are you going to get engaged?"

This is the "What's Next Syndrome." It is much easier to think about what is next rather than enjoying what is now. To be content in all seasons is not a matter of accumulating more, but a matter of valuing what you already have in front of you. When I look back on my college career, I realize something. I wish I had enjoyed it more. I wish I had enjoyed taking the classes, studying late nights, working on projects with a team, and studying abroad.

Humility changes your life because you begin to highly value today while you are on a trek for a better tomorrow.

The 3P's and Humility

Your purpose is not to make your name big or get a lot of money. Nor is it to have a significant position with a lot of influence. Nor is it to create a cocoon of self-sufficiency. You are already set with everything you need in life, today.

In his book, Money: Master the Game, Tony Robbins talks about figuring out what your exact, true, and calculated goal for financial success is. It's important to know, with clarity, what your goal is so that you can know when you reach it.

He recounts a moment in one of his seminars with a young man who said his idea of financial success is $1 billion.

Robbins loves drive and ambition, so he took the young man a step further. He asked him, what financial freedom would like if you did have $1 billion. The young man tossed out a few ideas—a private jet, luxurious cars, a grand home. Tony accepted and ran the numbers with this young man.

They soon came to realize that, instead of buying a jet, he could much more easily rent one and still do everything he loved. He could own the car for a relative monthly payment and get the house of his dreams. And he could do all this for less than $10 million.

That may still seem like a lot, but $10 million is much less than $1 billion.

Now, imagine you have $1 billion dollars in your bank account today, what would you do differently today? What would you stop doing? What would you start doing?

Would you quit your job, start a new company, hire an assistant, quit school, give your family all brand new homes, travel the world?

(You would be surprised at how many people don't have an answer to this question; yet, every day complain about their lot, their life, and their friends.)

Do you even need $1 billion? Okay, say you get everything you want. The immediate needs are satisfied, you bought your family a few homes, and you are settling into your new lifestyle, you still have $884 million left, what do you do now?

In the Kingdom, you can stop searching for more. When you search for more, you are saying I don't have enough and saying I need to do it on my own. You are saying you have a want. That only produces wanting. Unconsciously, that is pride because pride seeks more.

Do you need more or can you rest assured that you have all you need?

When you work from a place of gratitude, it stirs something entirely different. As Tony earlier describes in his book, some of the richest men on the earth work harder in their later years. They are not afraid of not having enough. Or, to compete to be the best. Because they can. That is what makes them purple cows.

Accept every humiliation, look at every single man who tries

or vexes you, as a means of grace to humble you.

Andrew Murray

When all kinds of trials and temptations crowd into your lives my brothers, don't resent them as intruders, but welcome them as friends! Realize that they come to test your faith and to produce in you the quality of endurance. But let the process go on until that endurance is fully developed, and you will find you have become men of mature character with the right sort of independence.

James 1 PHILLIPS

Go! Guide

This section below is an in-depth analysis of goal setting. Something that will push you to clarify your vision. Because, with a clarified vision, you have defined opportunities to building character. And purpose requires that you have a solid character. Remember there is additional material at purposebuiltyoung.com/resources.

When most people set out to achieve new goals, they ask, 'Okay, I have my goal; now what do I need to do to get it?' It's not a bad question, but it's not the first question that must be tackled either. The question we should be asking ourselves is: 'Who do I need to become?'

DARREN HARDY, *THE COMPOUND EFFECT*

Goal-Setting

For a moment, let go of all your current circumstances and take your most ambitious goal that you wrote before. Take that, and write down the top five goals you need to accomplish in the next fifteen years to reach those goals:

1. _____
2. _____
3. _____
4. _____
5. _____

Write your top two goals for each below. Identify these as six months to five-year goals.

Work (Mastery): What do you want to be best in the world at?

1. _____

2. _____

School (Education): What topics, languages, skills do you want to gain?

1. _____

2. _____

Personal: What would you enjoy having in life (excellent health, a strong family unit, etc.)

1. _____

2. _____

10× Your Goals

Once you have affirmed your goals and why you have set those goals, I want you to experiment. In the book 10X, Grant Cardone tells an interesting lesson. He realized, throughout life, every time he would achieve a goal, he would always surpass it.

Often I hear people say, I would never have imagined this would happen. From struggling to eating one healthy meal a week to being called a fitness guru, people often dream smaller than what they are capable. That is to say, we base our dreams on what we want to overcome, not our full potential.

Rather than setting your goals on just taking the next step in your life (even though that is super important), I want you to take your six goals above and multiply them by ten. Dream big. Imagine what you can do in light of the fact that most people surpass their goals. Write them below:

Work (Mastery): What do you want to be best in the world at?

1. _____

2. _____

School (Education): What topics, languages, skills do you want to gain?

1. _____

2. _____

Personal: What would you enjoy having in life (excellent health, a strong family unit, etc.)

1. _____

2. _____

The Character Required

Finally, it is time to take what Darren Hardy so eloquently wrote and was quoted at the beginning of this Go! Guide to bring it to life. If you want to have better health, you have to take more responsibility for your health. That requires character growth. The question isn't just what do you want to do, but who do you want to be? What are your goals calling for you? For example, a doctor needs a character of high ethical responsibility to care for his patients and protect the medical industry. A teacher needs a selfless spirit. What will your goals call for you to become?

→ _____

_____

_____

Once you complete this task, seek feedback. Tell a mentor or friend—someone who believes in you—with full transparency what you are trying to achieve. Discuss what you will accomplish in the next six months to five years.

Exiting the Atmosphere of your Comfort Zone

We often refer to our comfort zone with much discussion and little explanation. Let's take a look at the forces behind our comfort zone.

Your comfort zone is anything you find easy to do. Either you have done it before, or you have done it so many times that this new experience is not so much different. Your comfort zone is what keeps your heart rate normal.

Imagine a circle, and at the center of that circle is the core of your comfort zone.

Stepping out of our comfort zone is just as difficult as defying nature. Our minds and bodies will do everything they can to resist stepping outside the comfort zone. Just like the gravitation force that keeps us on the ground, our comfort zone is drawing us toward what is simple, easy, and understood.

Our comfort zone has a best friend, the path of least resistance. They hang out all the time. If you meet one, you are more likely right next to the other. They are like identical twins who share clothing and their toothbrush. They get along very well.

The core center of your comfort zone is strong enough to pull you toward it even when you know the path is destructive or harmful. This is why people stay in unhealthy relationships too long, can't let go of bad eating habits, or are too afraid to try something new. The gravitation force of our comfort zone has one objective: to keep us in the familiar even if it may be better for us to step out.

That's why most people rather fit in than stand out. Standing out confronts our comfort zone. That's why most people settle for mediocre, follow the status quo, give up on their dreams, and settle. Pushing against this resistance makes our comfort zone exposed and vulnerable. And our comfort zone does not want to become exposed and vulnerable. Vulnerability is the only way you build love and service.

To operate outside of your comfort zone, one of three things must happen (or a combination of all three).

You Are Forced Out

You lose a job. Your girlfriend breaks up with you. You have to move across the country. You have to have a job. You get behind on payments toward your credit card. You are forced to do something that you may not be so interested in doing.

You Are Miserable

You dread going to class. It takes every ounce of effort to make it to your 11:00 a.m. course. You sit there, inattentive, even a bit angry at what is happening. You are in a relationship that seems to be dealing with more arguments than love, more yelling than holding hands, and more pain than joy. You are sitting in a cubicle, supposed to be working, but you are reading this book. You are miserable. Your boss doesn't care two licks about your future. Your boss won't listen to your input. You are undervalued and overworked.

You feel miserable most of the day.

You Initiate

Simply put, you willingly step out of your comfort zone. You take responsibility to go beyond the path of least resistance. To initiate is much more of a forward, free action than the other two. This option is where most people fall short. This is why so many people settle for mediocre lives. They willingly give in to their comfort zone.

Here is the interesting part, though, of how our comfort zone works. Our comfort zones are not biased toward our destruction; they are biased on safety. In other words, our comfort zones could hold us back or can propel us forward. It all depends on what we deem as safe.

Think of it this way. My comfort zone tells me not to get on the dance floor and dance. But when I willfully ignore its advice and march directly on the dance floor and unleash, at a certain point, I am drawn to the safety of a different zone.

If our comfort zone is a circle with a gravitation force, then, to escape that gravitational force, we must push against gravity. As we struggle against gravity, the entire time, our minds will be telling us to retreat, go back to comfortable, this is dangerous, don't do this, you don't know what's out there if you leave orbit you may die! Comfort zones are very dramatic.

The entire time we are in the circumference of our comfort zone, it pulls us toward the center. But the moment we enter orbit, and we have left the atmosphere, we enter an entirely new arena. To do this, we need what scientists call escape velocity.

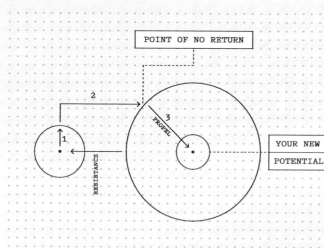

Visual 4: Comfort Zone Challenges
You go from one gravitation atmosphere bent toward your comforts, past, and weakness to another world of redefined strength and possibility.

Escape Velocity

The escape velocity to exit the earth's orbit is at least 25,000 mph. That is seven miles per second. At that speed you can fly from New York to California in less than six minutes. All that to say, the speed is fast. And the speed is not just about the quickness; it is about energy.

You can never get rid of your comfort zones. It's about escaping the demise of any given comfort zone.

When you begin to step out of your comfort zone, your brain reacts with negative, counter arguments on why you should raise the white flag and turn back. At a certain point, and this is relative to everyone, you exit the atmosphere of the first comfort zone.

There you meet space. It is wide and empty. A bit confusing, open, and ambiguous. Here is what we can call the transition period. This space you meet while stepping out of our comfort zone is often very short and unnoticed, but it still exists. You can still retreat up to this point.

Then you hit the point of no return. This happens when you touch the new atmosphere you are entering. It is completely new and different from the previous atmosphere. In the same way that the first atmosphere had a gravitational pull towards the core, this one does as well. You are getting drawn into the new central zone. That is, if you have ever been nervous of dancing on the dance floor (in comfort zone #1), you get on the dance for a bit nervous (hit space), and then are feeling so comfortable showing off all your bedroom moves (comfort zone #2), you know what I am talking about. You are not only dancing on the dance floor, but you are dancing around the tables, on your way to the bathroom, and on your drive home in the car. You go from being exceptionally afraid to exceptionally alive.

Meet comfort zone number two: this is what I like to call your new potential. You have just discovered a new ability or skill or talent or endurance.

You go from one gravitational pull of weakness and vulnerability to another, in a new atmosphere of strength and possibility.

That is why I said, your comfort zones are not biased. They just act accordingly. They act in one way. You can either be destroyed by it or leverage it.

We are drawn into what we know, as with such forces of gravity that we often do not see when our comfort zones are leading to more destruction than potential.

The most critical step to your success often comes when you make a decision to go into uncomfortable situations willingly. Often, that is when you confront fear at the highest level. Like when you go on the dance floor, even though your heart is pounding.

Your New Potential

I remember this point coming alive while I was traveling and starting a new part of my journey. I was leaving Berlin after living there for two and a half months. I was going to Spain to spend a week there. When I was departing from everything I had recently come to know as my home, I started to feel that this next leg of the journey would be dreadful. I began to reminisce and think of all the fun I had during that trip to Berlin. Then, as soon as I got to the airport and was sitting right beyond the security check at my terminal (the point of no return), I realized how excited I was for the next leg.

It wasn't until reaching the point of no return did I feel right about the next part of the journey.

The same thing happened when I was departing from Myanmar to go to Singapore. I had just spent three full weeks in Myanmar doing fabulous ministry over Christmas and New Year's Day. The day before my departure flight, I was extremely sick. By that point, I just wanted to go home. I knew I had enjoyed a lot already.

After I left my local guides, checked in, went through security, and sat at the terminal for my flight to Singapore, I realized something. My spirit had shifted. I was full of energy and life. I had entered a new atmosphere.

Both of these moments I was forced to do it. When I started this book, I was miserable in my current comfort zone.

Meet your new potential by stepping through your comfort zone. It sometimes takes multiple visits to make your new potential a lifestyle, the same way it takes twenty-one days to create a habit. When you have brought in your new potential, you then start to realize what God has in store for you.

Wouldn't it be interesting to know that Earth and Venus are close in proximity and relatively the same size. yet they are the exact opposite? Our comfort zones are misleading if we don't realize, they may look safe, but sometimes, there comes a point where you have to leave one to move to the next. Not because it is evil. Rather, because it's time for you to step into a new atmosphere.

Your dreams often come by a chase. To pursue your dreams, you must step outside your comfort zone. This process then repeats over time, again, in a healthy cycle.

Comfort Zone Challenges

It's healthy to push against your comfort zone every day, whether it is in a major way or a minor way. What keeps 90 percent of people away from large steps of faith and a lack of trust? They never take the small steps. The thinking goes like this: I am not ready to take the big step of faith, so the small step is seemingly unimportant. This is where fear steps in and agrees that inaction is a good option. Challenging our comfort zone will allow us to push beyond the confines of fear.

Every comfort zone challenge is made to confront your fear. You will fall. You will fail and you will suffer setbacks. That is not a problem. That is something good. What makes this life worth living is expanding so that our space is open. When our space is open, we have room to let God come and work, and when we leave that room open, we are ready to love and serve others as they call.

Each of these will make you better at initiating. And the better you are initiating, the better you become at everything you face in life. You take responsibility, you grow, and most of all, you have authenticated your faith, a necessary skill today.

If you struggle to face big fears, it's good to have a daily practice of facing smaller fears (i.e., your comfort zone). So that, when it comes time to pioneer, you are well able to confront the uncomfortable situations. Here are a few ways of doing that:

Don't forget there is additional material at purposebuiltyoung.com/resources.

> It is not because things are difficult that we do not dare; it is because we do not dare that they are difficult.
> LUCIUS ANNAEUS SENECA, ROMAN PHILOSOPHER, STATESMAN, AND ORATOR

Wake Up Before You Should

This is just a good practice in any life. Give yourself the sense of accomplishment before you even begin. Wake up earlier, thank God for the day, read one verse of scripture, stretch... Do something! This will start your day with a sense of accomplishment. Something you chose to do. This will give you a positive impact for the rest of your day. Create two wins in the first ten minutes of your day (drink a bottle of water, thank God for life, write one thought, something).

Your Personal Wake-Up Call

Some of you will love this one and some will hate it. During your shower, turn the water ice cold! Embrace it for twelve seconds. Feel all your cells come alive as they react to the frigid temperatures. Don't worry, after twelve seconds turn it back warm.

The Art of Saying a Polite No

Take a month where you decline all extra-curricular activities. When you are invited for coffee, out to eat late at night, or on a last minute plan, unless you have a strong compulsion to go, say "no." Use the small NOs to make room for the big YES. This may help prepare you for a transformative season in your future where you will need to say a big no for an even bigger yes in your future.

Challenge Your Ego

Give: Next time you are given your favorite expensive box of chocolate desserts instead of keeping it, give it away. There is something so powerful when we take something that we receive and value and freely give it away.

Serve: Once and a while, give up your rights and do what someone asks you. It doesn't matter if you are right. It doesn't matter if you know a more efficient way of doing something. Give others space to grow. Let others make a mistake.

Love: Submit to your most dreaded relationship. If you have a bad boss, a tyrant parent, or a demeaning sibling, learn to love them unconditionally. Not because you are weaker or less significant. Rather, learn where they are and do one thing that helps improve their life.

Remember, you will never cut your values in this time. Instead, you will be building your values. Because, whatever you value will cost you something. If you value high-quality customer service, it may cost you extra time and money over the phone with local farmers to stock the kitchen with the best quality products. In the same way, if you value your relationship with God, it will cost you time and energy. It will cost you bearing the brunt of people's mistakes and life's challenges.

If you are unemployed for a season, a real test of humility, try and continue to engage life with love and energy. This type of radical approach makes time seem valuable, in every season.

Each of these tests will confront your worst fears and then ask, just like Seneca asked, "Is this the worst condition that I feared?"

Doubt

Faith and doubt cannot exist in the same mind at the same time, for one will dispel the other.

THOMAS S. MONSON, CLERGYMEN

Which career path should you choose? Which route should you take? Who should you marry? Will you start a business? What goals are worth embracing?

Many of lifes most important questions require us to have faith. Certainly, our highest calling will require faith. To realize our dreams, we must step out in our Grind Faith.

While I was writing, I met up with Edwin Lai to have coffee. Edwin is a young professional. Inside of Edwin, he was feeling an itch pushing him toward a new direction. He had a stable job, a stable relationship, and a stable household.

He told me that his relationship had just ended. A few days after that his landlord communicated that his family would have to move out. They only had a few weeks to relocate.

And before either of these situations arose, he felt a strong impression to tell his supervisor that he would be leaving his job soon. By the way, he had no idea where he was going next.

Everything in his life that gave him stability in a short, quick period came crashing down.

What keeps us from going in the direction we most desire?

It is most often doubt. Doubt, in its usual 'common sense' approach, will do its work to keep us from fully exploring an uncertain future.

How do we have faith to believe every day, when there may be little to no evidence that we are heading in the right direction?

For Edwin, it wasn't about getting rid of the uncertainty. That day at the coffee shop he showed remarkable peace and calmness, despite everything in his life being in flux.

The future will always be uncertain. *Always.*

It was his ability to have Grind Faith.

The truth is, the ones who are faith-filled are the ones that have colossal *faithless* moments.

Introduction

There's no evidence for God; There's no life after death; there's no absolute foundation for right and wrong; there's no ultimate meaning for life; and people don't really have free will.

WILLIAM PROVINE, CORNELL UNIVERSITY

Everything about faith can be summarized by this quote. Faith is believing, whatever you believe. Because what you believe, you set into motion in your life—whether positive or negative.

And one must be able to have the ability to walk out their faith through the storms of life.

Grind Faith—the daily steps of faith into our dreams, desires, and calling—is not on a winning streak. Faith isn't about blindly following the words of the Bible. Faith isn't a multiple choice test where you aim to get an A+. Faith requires you to map a person-specific journey from your current circumstances to the best version of you.

The best part of building your Grind Faith? You take away all the power of the devil. How much ground does the devil have in your life during challenging situations when you respond by growing? Very little! Continuous improvement counters everything the devil will try and disrupt in your life.

Grind Faith

Everything is possible for one who believes.

JESUS MARK 9 NEW INTERNATIONAL VERSION (NIV)

Then he touched their eyes, saying, "According to your faith be it done to you.

JESUS, MATTHEW 9

Supersize Me

After Jesus had fed the 5,000 men, walked on water, and told the great parables around the streets of Israel, a gentile woman (foreigner to Israel) asked Jesus for help. She said, "Have mercy on me, O Lord, Son of David; my daughter is severely oppressed by a demon." Jesus answered, "I was sent only to the lost sheep of the house of Israel." His answer, however, seems to have a tone of agitation. This was unlike Jesus, and it is much more unlike most of the stories we read in the gospels describing Jesus.

Consider that Jesus was seemingly kinder with the crippled man and the salvation of the harlot who was about to be beaten.

When it came to this women, however, her plead was refuted by Jesus saying, "It is not right to take the children's bread and throw it to the dogs."

I'm not sure what Jesus was saying here. As if her desire to heal her daughter was incongruent with the heart of God or that Jesus was asking for her to have bigger faith.

She makes the second plea and says, "Yes, Lord, yet even the dogs eat the crumbs that fall from their masters' table."

In the end, Jesus spells out the value of big faith. In Matthew 15, it reads, "O woman, great is your faith! Be it done for you as you desire." Her daughter was healed instantly.

My first takeaway from this story is don't give up so quickly. It may be hard, but not impossible. Preserve. Endure. Have tenacity. Push for what you believe. Jesus acknowledges that her faith is great by way of her ability to believe. Thus, have big faith!

Sometimes when we ask Jesus for something, it happens quickly. Other times it happens once we commit. Other times, it doesn't happen for years. In any case, it begins once we push beyond some initial constraints and demonstrate bigger faith.

Supersize me, please.

The Only Pen I Use

The only pen I use is a Pilot G-2 .38. I don't like writing with the .5 and definitely not anything thicker. I am left-handed, therefore, when I write, if the ink doesn't dry quickly, I end up smearing everything on the page.

Anyhow, two chapters later, the book of Matthew recounts another story.

The disciples had just returned from praying for the sick and casting out demons. The first 'mission trip' of its kind. In theory, the disciples knew this stuff worked. They should have been able to follow Jesus' commands and come back with some amazing Jesus-moving-mountain stories. Plus, they had an advantage; they saw Jesus do the miracles we read about today. Then, on the mission field, when they attempted to pour our God's power, all that came was a backfire. They prayed to cast out the demon from a boy and nothing happened. Christ had given them this power.

Not much to show for everything they had witnessed.

Then, the boy's father approaches Jesus. He needed to make his plea with someone with more authority. This man's son was possessed, and the man asks Jesus for mercy. Jesus, a bit frustrated with the current state of things, makes his point by healing the boy, instantly.

The disciples, taken aback by this charity that they were unable to perform, ask unselfishly, "why couldn't we do that?"

"Because of your little faith," Jesus responded.

To our surprise, what Jesus says next is striking and nearly anyone who has attended a few services would know these exact words.

Jesus said to have faith the size of a mustard seed, and you can move mountains.

But, didn't He just tell them their faith is too small? Jesus said your faith it too tiny, that is why you cannot heal this boy. Apparently, their faith was smaller than a mustard seed. He then says you need faith the size of a mustard seed. A mustard seed? Have you seen a mustard seed? It is so tiny! It is half the size of an orange seed and not much bigger than the tip of a ball-point pen. It's the same size of the tip of my favorite pen.

Jesus just made it clear: Faith, the size of a tip of a ball point pen, would make nothing impossible.

Well, Which One is It?

Should our faith be big or small? Should we be living with a small, medium, or XX-large faith? The first story summarizes a situation requiring big faith. Then the second story tells of faith equivalent to the size of a mustard seed.

Maybe the stories are situational. At times, you need bigger faith and other times not so much. Both have power. The only problem with this conclusion is that both the miracles, on the outside, appear the same. They were both casting out demons.

What if you even compare the miracles and how they came about? The woman was a foreigner to the land, a gentile. She had few rights in Israel. Is this a gentile thing? As a foreigner, one has to do more to receive God's blessing?

On the other hand, the disciples were just trying to release a young boy (representing a lot of innocence) from being demon-possessed. It was their first solo journey. The disciples were ready to come back with some amazing stories from their mission trip. This was a perfect training season. Then, when they are unable to do the miracle, all of a sudden, Jesus does it, instantaneously!

Plus, He metaphorically connects this moment to having the same power of moving a mountain. Isn't moving a mountain more strenuous than casting out a demon?

Is this a gender thing?

Is this a mood thing?

Hardly the conclusion we could draw.

Size

We know faith is not about being big or small. It's about the *object* of your faith.

Imagine you walked into my home to stay there for a few days. I invited you and told you I have a place for you to sleep and store your things while you explore the town. When you arrived, I informed you that your bedroom is just down the hallway. You see the hall. I begin to tell you that there is a well-furnished queen size bed, desk, and dresser. If you believe I am telling the truth, you have faith because you have yet to see the items.

Do you believe in the bed, the desk, and the chair or do you believe in me?

"Precisely, which is why the next step is to *clarify the object* of your faith," Lynn Anderson, who wrote *If I Believe, Why do I have these Doubts*, told Lee Strobel during an interview.

"We Canadians know there are two kinds of ice,'" he continued, "'thick and thin. You can have very little faith in thick ice, and it will hold you up just fine; you can have enormous faith in thin ice, and you can drown. It's not the amount of faith you can muster that matters up front. It may be tiny, like a mustard seed. But your faith must be invested in something solid.'"

Now, imagine again I took you into my house and asked you what you believed was in the bedroom, before I illustrated what was in there. Maybe you said a similar set of items—a bed, a desk, and a place to keep clothes.

Well, up until that point, that is your guess. It is your opinion. You believe those items may be there (the same way you believe that the future will be bright, provided for, and enjoyable). But, your faith is not in the bed, the dresser, or a desk, it is again in me—the person who brought you to the room.

In other words, it is in God. Not in a job you are hoping for, a house you want to live in, a ministry that flourishes, or for the right relationship. It must be solely in God. Those things reflect the beauty of our Creator, but we do not put our faith in those particular items.

It isn't a mistake that the Bible talks about faith the size of a mustard seed or the greatest faith in Israel. It isn't a mistake that our hearts desire to have faith in something. What is important is how we live it out.

Faith

Matthew 15 and 17 are not in conflict. What is happening in this story is that Grind Faith is beginning to take on a new role on Jesus' terms. Not to miss sight of the definition of faith in Hebrews 11, we will use a simple definition here: **initiate your walk *towards* God.**

You believe in something. That means you have faith in something. Grind Faith is carried in everything you do from taking customer orders at work to praying. Every day, you probably don't question if salvation is real or if your experiences with Jesus are real. Rather, the questions of faith come in believing God in the midst of a storm, during a season of expansion, and in the uncertainty of life.

My Faith

There, on every church website, is a list of the tenets of faith. The tenets of faith are the pillars the church represents like God is triune, Jesus is the Son of God, Jesus died and rose again, miracles still happen today, and a few more.

To believe God is triune is easier for me than to believe that Jesus is real. That He is the Son of God is simple for me, too. When it comes to miracles, I struggle. When it comes to believing every chapter of the Bible, I struggle, too.

We can easily build walls between ourselves and others (ministries, churches, faith-based organizations, and people) by this almost subconscious pattern of faith. When, for the average person, it is difficult to believe all the tenets of faith, all the time.

Many (not all) teach an 'if you take one you get them all' type of faith. Of course, I am not saying we can separate these truths.

Instead, realize that faith is more about *developing* a set of beliefs rather than a one-size-fits-all uniform. It's a personalized journey.

For me, believing in miracles and understanding that the entire Bible is holy took time. I am still learning to believe. To see people come to Jesus, experience healing, and pray for the sick took stages. To see the stories from the tower of Babel to the rebuilding of the wall to the stories of Paul's missionary journey as part of God's holy word required thoughtful prayer and devotion to fully believe.

The point is this: Jesus is more interested in people who can be real about their current situation and what they believe than to wear a superficial persona of faith.

Exam

In a perfect world, my college career would have been marked with well-thought-out scheduling and preparation for exams and papers. I would study weeks in advance. Know the testable material from cover to cover and even be able to pose interesting topic conversations around the course content. During my years of study, this was seldom the case. I studied last minute, with late nights and early mornings, trying to cram five chapters of information into my mind for an hour of mental vomiting onto the page. It was the best I, and many other students, could do with busy schedules and loads of information to consume.

When taking a multiple choice exam, you learn some of the tricks of the trade. You become a better test-taker. You find out how to eliminate the definite wrong answers first. Then, read each question carefully to make sure that one part of it is not off-base. If it is, you eliminate that answer as well. You compare. You jot all the notes in your head. Then, if you are still unsure, you go to the first answer you felt in your gut was accurate. If all else fails, go for C!

Our faith is not supposed to be like a multiple choice exam. You cannot study, prepare, or rehearse to get every question right. Preparation is highly important for us so we can do our best during the exam. Even more so, it is not only to get the right answer, so you can say you have an A+ in life. It's not about having all the answers right. It's the continual decision to believe. Not to be perfect or never make a mistake. On the contrary, because you probably will fail often. Failure is not bad. It is not (and this will be important for some of you) tied to making a mistake. Just because you failed doesn't mean you are a loser or not going the right way. It tends to mean that you are trying.

(Plus, waiting in life for the answer could be deadly.)

With heart, faith is a constant decision to continue to step forward (initiating your walk towards God), whether you know the answer or guess C.

Creativity, Faith, and Life

No good e'er comes of leisure purposeless;
And heaven ne'er helps the men who will
not act
SOPHOCLES (497 BC)

At 14-years-old Easton LaChappelle built his first robotic arm out of Legos. Over time, he improved his design to the point where he could use a 3D printer and operate the arm without touching it.

One day he was at a science fair and encountered a 7-year-old girl with a prosthetic arm. He learned that the arm cost her parents $80k, and she would grow out of it soon and need another one.

He was inspired and dared to turn his prototype into a scalable and affordable device. Five years later, LaChappelle produced a prototype for less than $1,000.

Now, the 7-year-old girl, and young children like her all around the world, could get a prosthetic for only $350.

"No one person can change the world," LaChappelle said in an interview. "It takes multiple people, so if I can develop technology in a way so other people can take what I've done and grow from it and do something more with it, someone could take that and keep impacting someone else's life and eventually try and rule out a lot of the bad in the world by giving back to our own kind."

Our appetite for faith is what makes us want to build, create, design, and be someone. If writing a book, preaching a sermon, building a business that aids tens of thousands of people is what your heart desires, then you will utilize many resources along the way. But the resources are not what you need. What you need is faith.

If you are alive, you are a creator. Don't get caught up in what the world defines as creativity. If you have a life (that is all you need), you are creative. Purpose, as it is unconditional, by God's amazing design, fashions us to want faith. Our faith is best built and joined to who we are when we create.

Creating brings one in direct contact with life. You should always be intentionally creating something. That way, you are deliberately rendezvousing with life. This daily practice makes you confront your true inner being and bring out the best you have. This type of thinking is much different to the world's look on living and creating. That is why this is done by faith. Call it creative leadership, lifestyle design, or intentional living; our Creator made us creative.

That is why we must confront doubt. Doubt will stand in the way of our faith. In Latin, they say 'Audentes Fortuna Adiuvat.' That is, fortune comes to the aid of those daring.

Creative Living

"So this, I believe," Elizabeth Gilbert writes in her book Big Magic, "is the central question upon which all creative living hinges: Do you have the courage to bring forth the treasures that are hidden within you?"

When Eric Liddell decided to opt out of his best event and race the 400m, he was not planning on breaking a world record. When Martin Luther hammered the ninety-five theses to the doors of the church, he did not set out to restructure the next 300 years of the church hierarchy. When Easton LaChappelle decided to create a scalable and affordable prosthetic, he was not intending on having the President of the United States shake it.

Each of these people stepped into the courage

it took to bring forth the work that was within them. The work that was critical. The work that would elevate humans to a new level of achievement.

They stepped into their Grind Faith.

Faith and The Impossible

Many will say it's impossible until it's done. Let's start the conversation the other way around.

It's possible. What has not yet been done is possible.

What is not yet done is what makes faith, faith. It's what makes it fun.

> "What we can or cannot do, what we consider possible or impossible, is rarely a function of our true capability.
> It is more likely a function of our beliefs about who we are."
> ANTHONY ROBBINS

Will we ever stop doing the impossible? I believe not. Remember our story about a young Eric Liddell who ran the 400m in the 1924 Olympic Games in Paris and his record time was 47.6. That was an unheard of speed at the time. In 1996, Michael Johnson set the world record at 43.49 seconds. That is four seconds faster! Up until early 2016, that record has yet to be broken.

In 1998, Ben Lecomte swam across the Atlantic Ocean. That is some 3,700 miles! It took seventy-three days of six-hour swims. His next feat is to swim from Tokyo, Japan to San Francisco, California. That is eight hours of swimming a day at forty miles a day.

Martin Luther was accused of mistranslation and condemned for trying to bring his perspective on the church. Steve Jobs was ridiculed for being so passionate about pressing the status quo. Ralph Lauren made his first ties out of rags—who would ever believe a poor immigrant in New York could change the fashion industry? Now many people who worked under Lauren have pushed fashion beyond anyone's wildest ideas, and at the same time, there are about thirty sub-brands under the Ralph Lauren hood that stock large department stores around the world.

You are constructed to build, create, and design. Faith is having fun in the possibility of doing the impossible.

Culture Asks

Only in a world where faith is difficult, can faith exist!

LEE STROBEL, A FORMER ATHEIST, TURNED FAITH-FILLED BELIEVER.
AUTHOR OF *THE CASE FOR FAITH*

In 2004, nine out of ten people had a landline in their home. That is down by almost 50 percent just ten years later in 2014. Landlines have not been lost, they have just been replaced.

For centuries, average people like you and me were unable to read the Bible. The clergymen—only a few—were the only ones to read and interpret the Bible.

Centuries before, the Bible wasn't the Bible, as we know it today. It was a set of scrolls. It was a set of teachings that were passed through the art of storytelling and tradition.

Centuries before that people were only allowed to come in contact with God through a high priest.

What holds us back from faith today?

It is not a literacy issue. Many can read, and if not, you can listen to a recording of the Bible.

It is not the Bible. We have it in the palm of our hands, and everywhere we go, and in more languages than ever before.

It is no longer a high priest. In Jeremiah, it says so clearly, if you seek Me with all your heart, you will find Me. Then what causes people of all cultures to lose faith?

They don't.

Faith is not lost; it has just been replaced.

Faith for Everything

In some developing nations when a family needs food, they must pray for God to provide it. In some developed nations, when a family needs food, they can pull out a credit card (or call a friend or sign up for government aid).

When our daily necessities no longer require faith, faith becomes an option. We replace faith with objects outside of God (a credit card, a government program, or a paycheck).

We always have faith in something. Moses had faith when he parted the Red Sea and when he struck the rock twice— even though the second strike was against God's command. Certainly, he had faith in God when he struck the rock the first time as God had commanded him. He had faith in his experience when he struck the rock again.

For everything we do, we have faith. It could be small or large. In either case, we can replace faith with a credit card, a friend, a government program, a salary, or a job. The challenge is having faith in the right object.

The Responsibility of Faith

On Christmas Eve in 1997, an episode of Sesame Street aired called Roy. Big Bird is immediately thrown into confusion once he discovers that his name is just a description of himself. He thinks of his friends named Oscar, Elmo, or Snuffy; their names are unique.

At that moment, he begins a wild search for a proper name. He asks his friends for suggestions. He gets Sammy, Butch, Bill, Omar, Napoleon, Rocky and more. He settles on Roy.

Everyone starts calling him by his new name. He soon realizes that he does not like Roy at all. He goes back to wanting to be called Big Bird.

Big Bird says, "Even if Big Bird isn't a regular name, it's my name, and I like the way all my friends say it."

Sometimes, our faith is something we have to explore for ourselves. It may not end up anywhere new, but the exploration teaches a life lesson. We can start where we will end up. Either way, skipping the journey is not an option. Our responsibility – to be intentional about our relationship with God – is what makes faith, faith. Living by faith may lead you in and out of something just to help you discover self-confidence and purpose.

Identify what you may struggle to believe and take full responsibility for it. For instance, if you struggle with believing in miracles, take the responsibility of learning about miracles, believing God does miracles, and documenting the stories that come along—both the positive and negative. Assuredly, you will grow.

Do You Tithe?

For a season of my life, I struggled with tithing. It wasn't because I didn't trust God. I was just confused.

I saw lots of money being spent on superfluous items and a disproportional smaller amount on the poor. It made me doubt what my tithe meant. Then, to complicate the situation, I began to ask, what verses in the Bible actually tell me I should tithe. I was confused by the entire 'storehouse' idea.

[In Malachi 3, the verse reads, "Bring the full tithe into the storehouse..."]

This led to a nine-month study on tithing and the practice of not tithing. I studied the scriptures, read books about the topic, and talked to mentors about it. I prayed and spoke to God about it directly. When I began to tithe again, I did exactly what I had been doing before. This time, however, it was my *own* faith. It was a personal decision.

We don't all have to do this, but we all have to do this: confront our person-specific doubts and decide to continue to believe, despite our doubt. We have to have faith that is genuine. We have to know why we show up each week to church, tithe, and obey as believers. Otherwise, it is blind following.

Overall, it all doesn't have to make sense now. It just needs to be your faith. Therefore, it's okay if you struggle with something. It might be that God is trying to reveal something to you or call you to action in a certain area of your life. Just like Big Bird, we may not have ended up anywhere new, but we learned a valuable lesson in the journey.

Blind (Without Reason)

Faith is not wishful thinking. It is ruled by reason. Take for example the theories of the Big Bang, the 'no-god' creation story, and evolution. In this book, *The Case for Faith*, Lee Strobel interviewed Walter Bradley, a highly sought after scientist. Bradley deflates these hard to understand topics with a simple study of probability. It seems that, even after billions of years that the earth can have potentially existed, it would not be enough time for Random Chance (the idea that, with enough time, chemicals will eventually create life), to occur.

"'And not only was the time too short, but the mathematical odds of assembling a living organism are so astronomical that nobody still believes that random chance accounts for the origin of life. Even if you optimized the conditions, it wouldn't work... the odds of creating just one functional protein molecule would be one chance in a 10 with 60 zeros after it,'" Bradley explained.

"'The probability,'" Bradley continued, "of linking together just one hundred amino acids to create one protein molecule by chance would be the same as a blindfolded man finding one marked grain of sand somewhere in the vastness of the Sahara Desert—and doing it not just once, but three different times."

You will always have faith in something—science, a boyfriend, or God—you are sure to put your trust in something. When you guess what is in the room, you (consciously or subconsciously) put faith in me. All that to say, your faith in God is not blind; rather, a believer walks in supreme certainty.

"Sir Frederick Hoyle put it colorfully when he said that this scenario is about as likely as a tornado whirling through a junkyard and accidentally assembling a fully functional Boeing 747,' Bradley concluded.

"Only a rookie who knows nothing about science would say science takes away from faith. If you study science, it will bring you closer to God."

Therefore, your faith doesn't have to rule away all reason (though a lot of things might not make sense in the physical realm, the Holy Spirit is there to guide you).

Roles of Faith

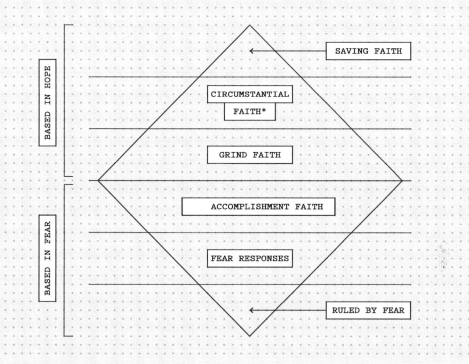

Visual 6: Faith Structure
*Circumstantial faith: Not faith that is only during certain circumstances, but faith that is graced during certain circumstances like cancer, sudden loss, or unexpected storms.

Our faith has six different roles. Or, if that seems hard to grasp, think of it this way. Your choice to have faith (or not have faith) in something appears in six different stages.

They are: Eternal Faith, Grind Faith, Circumstantial Faith, Achievement Faith, Fear Responses, and Ruled by Fear. Each of these is either rooted in hope or fear, what some philosophers have called the deepest two emotions we truly have.

Eternal Faith: Faith in salvation.

Grind Faith: Faith for your day-to-day circumstances that is always rooted in hope and what the Bible says about your life despite circumstances.

Circumstantial Faith: Faith for the hard seasons of life. You get fired or dumped. You are un- wanted by your family. You must live on an almost impossibly small paycheck. Faith that is given to you from a set of hard situations. One example would be Martin Luther King J as he led the Civil Rights movement upholding a nonviolent approach.

All these above are rooted in hope.

Achievement Faith: Faith based on if I do x, then I will get y.

Fear Responses: Doing something because you are afraid of something else. An example of this is when someone goes to church for the sole reason that they don't want God to smite them.

Ruled by Fear: This is the most pervasive and deadly. This is when you are completely run by fear. Life decisions are based on fear.

All these above are rooted in fear.

Realize that one action could come from either Grind Faith or Achievement Faith and look identical. The beauty of this model is in understanding the sole underlining key. Anything you do is either rooted in hope or fear. When you are stuck and cannot make a decision in life, maybe you have to discover what is behind that decision. Is it hope or fear?

The key is also knowing that every single thing you do is birthed in some level of faith. Faith is anything you do. Faith initiates you to walk toward (or away) from God. Thus, Achievement Faith, Fear Responses, and being Ruled by Fear are all faith in the wrong thing.

Challenger: Doubt

If faith never encounters doubt, if truth never struggles with error, if good never battles with evil, how can faith know its power? In my own pilgrimage, if I have choose between a faith that has stared doubt in the eye and made it blink or a naive faith that has never known the firing line of doubt, I will choose the former every time.

GARY PARKER, THE GIFT OF DOUBT

In the 2013 movie, *The Croods*, DreamWorks Animation brings to life a caveman family living in the canyon behind a rock. After their cave is destroyed, they are forced out of their comfort zone to face the unknown and uncertain world to find a new home. Then, the only way to move forward is to face their fears. They have no idea where they are going. Their biggest challenge is not the travel, potential threats, or finding food. Their biggest challenge is, as Seth Godin calls it 'the Dip;' creative circles call it the 'U-shape of creativity;' and we will refer to it as doubt.

The cavemen eventually recognize that they will have to overcome doubt and in the process realize that they have precisely what it takes to survive. It's the only way they will reach full potential.

In your life you will have to overcome doubt. The quicker you know that, the faster you will utilize the insight doubt gives you in any given situation about your unrealized value.

The Process

During the valley lows, doubt seems to cascade over much of life's hope and aspiration. We question our ability. We are afraid. Many people call this 'the process' (or the journey or 'life'). What the process does is leave us unsure of ourselves and that could be the most disenchanting reality.

The class that seems to bug you the most is not only wasting your time, but making you feel unsure of yourself. You butt heads with the co-worker who just doesn't understand and you feel like your personality isn't good enough. Your issues at home and with the family that makes you feel second class.

These places can be (and should be) redefined as the best process of life.

Seth Godin, in his book *The Dip*, says, "The people who set out to make it through the Dip—the people who invest the time and the energy and the effort to power through the Dip—those are the ones who become the best in the world. They are breaking the system because, instead of moving on to the next thing, instead of doing slightly above average and settling for what they've got, they embrace the challenge."

The U-shape of creativity states that every creative endeavor will have the highs and lows of a 'U.'

Doubt says, against your faith, you will be challenged with a lack of surety in the middle of the process.

This is the process. If you call it the 'U-shape of creativity,' the dip, or doubt, this is part of the journey.

Living by Faith

If it takes five years to earn the degree, the doubt will happen between years two and four. You will question: Am I going the right way? Is this worth it?

When pushing forward in a new family, the doubt will happen between unexciting years of marriage. Not on the wedding day or when the child is born. Doubt comes, at its heaviest, in the middle.

The good part is, you are built bigger than it. You have things within you and you don't realize it. You are equipped for the task at hand. It's your unrealized value. And living by faith is the surest way for you to realize the value inside of you.

How Doubt Works

It's simple.

Doubt doesn't happen at the end of a story (though it makes it feel like the end of the story).

Doubt doesn't occur at the spark of inspiration (though it's not a far off).

Doubt happens in the middle. It will always happen and its favorite time to show up is in the middle. It will use the 'insufficiency' around you to make you quit. It will use the scarcity within you to make you quit. Neither are good reasons to quit.

Doubt is completely internal. And, without a doubt, it shows up on your face as you speak, it reveals itself in your hands as you write, and it shows up in your step as you walk when it's roaring inside of you.

What you may fail to realize is that doubt is like a four-legged chair with only one leg. It's not as sturdy as it thinks.

Once you know this, you are already ten times more capable of beating it down.

Doubt

I'm unsure. I'm afraid. I'm not big enough. Not tall enough. Not short enough. Not outspoken. I'm not fun enough. Skinny enough. Old enough. Young enough. Inspired enough. Smart enough. Rich enough. Disciplined enough. Free enough.

Doubt will tell you, in whatever way, that you are not enough.

Paulo Coelho, the author of *The Alchemist*, shared on a podcast that his first publisher gave him back the rights to the book because it was unsuccessful. It had only sold 900 copies in the first year. At that point, he tells the listeners that there was a one-month span where he was about to quit altogether. Rather than quitting, he followed his dream to become a writer and found a publisher in the US (a difficult job for an unknown Brazilian author) to pick up the book. The book has now sold more than 65 million copies.

When you believe in yourself, you open the door for endurance, resilience, and tenacity. Some of the finest traits there are.

Doubt capitalizes on a lack of self-confidence. But, remember, that is all it has. It doesn't have any other triggers to pull when you believe that God made you *enough*.

Fovea Vision

Never quit something with great long-term potential just because you can't deal with the stress of the moment.
SETH GODIN, *THE DIP*

Fovea vision is your eye's ability to focus on a particular object when there are countless things to look at. At this moment, you are focused on the text of this book. That means you are not focused on looking around your room, the coffee shop, the hallway, or your feet, for that matter. What you focus on makes the difference. You cannot focus on two things at the same time.

You get through doubt in the most amazing way when you have fovea vision for your future. Fovea vision reminds you of why getting to the other side matters. Especially when challenges come, it's what drives you. If you don't have fovea vision or don't see the purpose in your life, you'll quit.

Imagine I offered you $2,000 to race a fifty-mile ultra-marathon. Chances are you might be inclined to start the training, but will give out by week two.

Instead, imagine if you were instructed to complete the fifty-mile race to raise $25k for your sister's heart surgery. How much more reason will you have to train?

People with incredible vision get through the Dip the best because they believe deep, deep down, despite doubt, that they will overcome the challenge.

Focus matters.

Listen to Yourself Grind

Our faith deals with our emotional fitness in many ways.

Say the following statements aloud:

I have great relationships with some of the most influential people on earth.

This year, I made more money than I had made in an entire lifetime.

With the help of a few organizations, we have come together to help nearly 1 million children left vulnerable find a home, education, and hope for their future.

I have just gone from leading a small start-up I founded to being a CEO with 350 employees and with $300 million in annual revenue.

Did any of those statements make you feel different? *That is because what we say affects who we are.* Your faith is what you *say* about yourself. Most of the time, we are giving ourselves the wrong messages. It is not about your emotions—being happy or sad—but having the emotional grit to believe what God says, despite your current circumstances. A person can live in complete freedom and have nothing, and a person could have everything and live in complete confinement. It all depends on what you say about yourself.

What Trials Reveal

What if every trial was meant to reveal to us a place in our lives that can use spiritual attention? Somewhat like a low gas indicator light coming on in your car. Our trials warn us of a place that is spiritually impoverished. A place for spiritual growth and improvement.

For instance, my neighbor, Eddie, is 38-years-old with two kids. At twenty-six, he rode his bike with a family member from San Francisco to San Diego—some 400 miles.

At twenty-nine years old, he was convinced by a friend to do it again. They hopped on a plane with their bikes, landed in SF, and in the airport parking lot, started the journey down south.

Both experiences, he recounted, were exhilarating and worthwhile.

But, both journeys didn't come pain-free. There were struggles, doubts, and trials that they had to work through.

However, when they finished, his friend mentioned that he was eager to do more with his life. He stepped up in his vocation, in his relationships, and in his capacity. The road he journeyed was a discovery of potential.

It revealed to him more potential than what he knew he had.

You are offered an opportunity, in every season of life to improve, grow, develop, and learn. When you go through a hard break-up, you are offered the position to rely on God to heal your heart. Your faith can grow and develop during a 'down' season.

In the same way, during the middle of a nonsense job, a position that seems to make no sense more than a paycheck, you can build the right heart stance toward people you don't enjoy working for and towards doing what is in front of you despite hating it.

In all, during any (every) season of life, you can build character. Start looking at how you can out-beat your current best.

All of our circumstances open a door for us to build our faith—both good and bad situations (especially the bad). When you grow during the difficult seasons of life, you unlock your potential. This is what I call your unrealized value.

Unrealized Value

The unrealized value of an individual comes when, despite life's dip, they continue to grow.

Unrealized value is when you begin to actually believe you have 10x value when you have only accomplished 2x results. It's when you aim after more than you ever have reached in your past because you believe God has more for you.

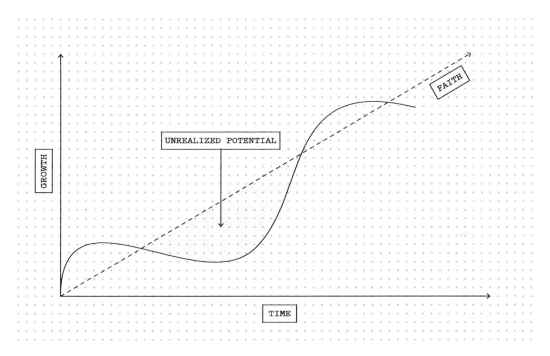

Faith
In every season of life you can always build faith. This chart shows how when we realize that we are confronted with doubt, in the middle of a dip, everything is telling us to quit. However, this is the most valuable growth we can achieve. It calls the most from us. It calls us to have faith in an unforeseen future despite our doubt.

Mute Them

The other day, I was on a conference call early in the morning with a few colleagues from around the globe. The beauty of the conference line is this: when you want to mute it, you can.

Doubt fills the mind and causes a lot of confusion and noise. The noise may not go away, and you may not be in a place to just walk away. But, what you can do is MUTE it.

Mute it quickly. Mute it again and again. Mute it when you just want to think for yourself. Mute it by changing your focus. Yes, they exist in the background, but let them. They have to get through their valuable charts and data and information.

You have the choice on how to incline your ear towards doubt.

Your Senses Matter

As you have seen, faith has much to do with your senses – what you see, say, and hear. You can control this more than you know to favor the outcome you desire. Spend ten or twenty minutes envisioning the future you want by closing your eyes and dreaming. Or, spend five minutes every morning reading to yourself a letter you write of affirmation. Or, listen to a motivational book or video for five to fifteen minutes in the morning. You can take one hour a day to spend building your faith. In every scenario, you are spending time in the future you want, despite your present circumstances. You are building your faith by aligning your focus to positive sights, sayings, and sounds.

How Does This Change Your Life?

Your job is not to leave a mark on earth but a mark on hell.

DAVID ISKANDER

During Aung San Suu Kyi's campaign in the late 1980s and early '90s, she made it clear, again and again, that her party was a non-violent campaign. She did not support the use of violence or weapons to sway others.

The government power, however, ruled with a heavy hand. At one gathering, while Aung San Suu Kyi's party was arriving, military forces were dispatched to end her campaign.

She was unaware of this. As her party began arriving at the location of the rally, Aung San Suu Kyi's team pointed on ahead. There, in their vantage, stood roughly ten soldiers with their weapons drawn.

Her party leaders instructed her to turn back. They had no weaponry. They had no self-defense. All they had was their lives that were now at stake. Right then, at that moment, Aung San Suu Kyi needed to make a decision. Everything in front of her told her to turn back. But, her vision gave her the exact power she needed to confront her doubt. She decided not to quit the long-term goal in the stress of the moment.

She had the blood of innocent young students who had rallied in August of 1988, and were ruthlessly killed by riot police, to think about. She had the staff, who were also ruthlessly murdered at Rangoon General Hospital, to think about. She had the innocent victims of police who ran senseless raids in the middle of the night arresting people unfairly to think about. Not to mention the death of her heroic father, who was assassinated by the hands of rebel groups. The same rebel groups that begun the military junta that she was now facing.

She was up against the exact enemy who had caused loads of pain for the 40+ million people of Burma. She was now facing what most would call the hardest challenge she had yet.

Shielded by her colleagues, Aung San Suu Kyi gently stepped forward, instructed her team to wait, and she calmly walked toward the soldiers.

Each step was a bold step of courage.

"Stop! You must turn back!" demanded the army commander who headed the troops.

She continued. Every step, a rightful step toward democracy.

Again the commander demanded, with adamant force, "You must turn back, or we will shoot!"

Aung San Suu Kyi took another step forward.

It was as if every step was a mark of courage and faith.

As if her father were there whispering in her ear, as he once had before, "Each and every one of you must make sacrifices to become a hero possessed of courage and intrepidity. Then only shall we all be able to enjoy true freedom."

Merit Never Works

You will never gain anything worthwhile if you expect anything. It's so counterintuitive, it's crazy. In truth, you will gain everything if you expect nothing.

If your faith is built on merit, you will feel a mess when things do not go your way. I have stayed away from the topic of 'works' because often the conversation is too far left. The conversation leaves people doing nothing because they would rather be 100 percent certain that they are not trying to 'earn' God's love than show forth effort in expanding God's Kingdom. It makes many people lazy. And, it makes James' lamentations cheap.

You cannot earn faith, but you cannot have faith without action.

Merited faith creates cultural Christians (churchgoing, Bible studying, passive individuals) as opposed to people who walk in security, identity, and objectivity.

Grind Faith allows you to embrace the nonsense of life while you make life meaningful. You stop searching for quick remedies and mitigating the pain with past solutions. You explore the depth of your pain. You do what's right before what is easy. You are committed to surrender and committed to overcoming.

Faith Pours Itself Out in Three Worlds

You live in three worlds at the same time. You choose how to balance the failures and successes of the past, how to enjoy the present, and at the same time be building for the future.

Live With the Past (World 1)

Life is lived forward but understood backwards.
KIERKEGAARD

Life is yours for the taking.

How can you improve, build, and grow?

Use your past to win today.

Believe, It's possible. Just believe.

Live in The Moment (World 2)

The master once said to his pupil, "When you walk, walk; when you eat, eat." The pupil said, "But doesn't everyone do that?" "No," the master said. "Many people when they walk are interested only in getting to the place where they are going. They are not really experiencing the walking. They don't even notice that they are walking. And many people, when they eat, are more involved in making plans about what they will do after they eat. This inattention to what they are doing means that they scarcely refer to what they are eating or to the fact they are eating. They are certainly not taking joy in the fact they are eating."[1]

You are not your past.

You are not your future, either.

Live fully, now.

You are, now.

Enjoy today.

Keep Moving Forward (World 3)

Life is lived moving forward.

It is not built on the past.

It is not built in the future.

Life is living moving forward.

It's a bit of a maze but it's worth every effort.

The Day the World Changed

Aung San Suu Kyi took another step forward. Now, she was only a few feet away from the barrels of each solider.

Her cry was for her people to attain the basic human rights they deserved. Nothing more.

The military commander ordered his troops with guns drawn to prepare to shoot. He began the countdown. "Stop! We have orders to kill you," he pleaded.

A countdown began.

"Five..." he yelled.

As she took another step closer, "Four!"

"Three!" Now, she was within inches of the barrel with her fate, her country, and her people's future at hand!

"TWO!"

All of the sudden, the commander began communicated on his radio.

"Stand Down!" He yelled in Burmese to his troops.

Something transpired that day in the streets of Myanmar that has come to affect the entire world. Aung San Suu Kyi, living with 'grace under pressure,' took one step of courage, just like the many tiny daily decisions she made, that led to a twenty-five-year fight for freedom. And without that one step, we have no idea where the fight for freedom in Myanmar would be today.

How does faith change your life? It takes mere moments and makes them meaningful. Faith gives the immense discoveries of science, technology, opportunity, democracy, and cultural norms significance. Faith takes our focus from doubt and sets our eyes on Jesus.

For we do not have a High Priest who is unable to sympathize and understand our weaknesses and temptations, but One who has been tempted [knowing exactly how it feels to be human] in every respect as we are, yet without [committing any] sin. Therefore let us [with privilege] approach the throne of grace [that is, the throne of God's gracious favor] with confidence and without fear, so that we may receive mercy [for our failures] and find [His amazing] grace to help in time of need [an appropriate blessing, coming just at the right moment].

Hebrews 4 AMP

Go! Guide

This section below is an in-depth analysis on making your goals practical. We will learn about the idea of duty, calling, and responsibility. Don't forget there is additional material at purposebuiltyoung.com/resources.

I believe in Christianity as I believe that the sun has risen: not only because I see it, but because by it I see everything else.

C. S. LEWIS, CHRISTIAN APOLOGIST

Duty, Calling, and Responsibility

To create beyond ourselves, everyone has three things they must address during every season of their life: Duty, Calling, and Responsibility.

Duty is what you have started and are obliged to finish by way of current assignment. This is different than calling, as calling is lifelong, duty is seasonal. As I write this, my duty is to focus on the edit and structural development of my first major publication. Once the book is completed, my duty will change accordingly.

Calling is a chosen craft, profession, or vocation. Something that is much bigger than yourself. If you had enough money, your life was in order, what would you do with your extra time? Whatever that would be, that is likely your calling. Calling is always connected to helping others. It could be building a craft, but that craft will always be tied to building others.

Responsibility is what you may or may not want to do. It is making sure the bills are paid. It's making sure that you care for your health in a season of busy work. It is when you set a time to work and a time to be with your family—so that they don't interfere with each other in a negative way. When duty and calling take a heavy load on your schedule what likely is to happen is that your responsibility will suffer. Responsibility sometimes falls in the mundane of life, but don't fret. There is always life worth recognizing and appreciating in the desert. It seems like a Herculean task at times, but it is what validates your calling all the more.

For instance, during the writing of this book, my duty was writing, my calling was to continue to be a voice for hundreds of orphans in Asia (something I am loyal to without having to try), and my responsibility was working my corporate career (even at times when I wanted to do one hundred other things with my time).

When you can incorporate all three modes in your season (and see how they fit together), you begin to realize where you move forward. The effect this system has is two-fold. First, in any season, your calling can become your duty or vice versa. These are not independent. When I started writing the book, I was answering my calling. During the process, my book became my duty to complete; I gave time, energy, and sacrificed other things for the production of this creative work.

Secondly, if you put all three on a scale of 100 percent, my duty was given 50 percent of my energy, my responsibility was given 25 percent of my energy, and calling was given 25 percent of my energy. Ironically, even as my duty took 50 percent of my energy, I was only able to give it 25 percent of my time. That is an entirely new conversation but definitely worth noting.

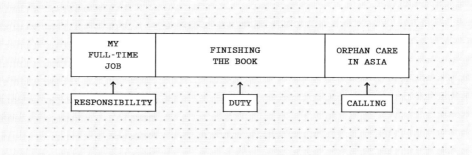

When you can minimize the responsibility category from taking 70 percent of your time, to, say, 30 percent of your time, you are winning. Now you have more time to fulfill your duty and calling. The more time you must spend to provide for your daily sustenance, the less time you give to fulfilling a calling that requires you to give of your time and services out of love.

Many people settle for little responsibility. They go to a job that tells them what to do and they take orders about everything they do. When it comes to being a pioneer, a funny thing happens. When you take more responsibility for your life, over time, you begin to have to give less and less of your time to your daily obligations.

The better you can line-up your duty, calling, and responsibility according to the season, the better shape you are in to own your future. Most people give 90 percent of their effort to a job that pays only enough to cover the bills. Most people get a college education-level of debt for the status symbol of a social norm that ties them to neglect their calling for five, ten, and twenty years.

To create beyond yourself, to have the freedom to be you and build the character you are capable of, outline below this season's duty, calling, and responsibility.

Duty:

→ _____

_____

Calling:

→ _____

_____

Responsibility:

→ _____

_____

Remember, this is seasonal. That means that this could change in three months or three years. The priority is understanding that you can be taking care of today, creating your future, and fulfilling a calling.

Envy

The sun said I want to be the earth—
look at all the people it inhabits and the way
it carries water and land.

The earth said I want to be the moon—look at how it
reflects the beauty of the sun so well and elegantly.
The moon said I want to be a star—look at how it
shines so bright, all by itself. The star said I want to be
a person—look at all the character they have to shine.
The person said I want to be God—look at how he
commands the whole universe as he pleases.

God said I want you to be you so that I can be
with you.

DAVID ISKANDER

Envy misappropriates the value of oneself. Envy makes all
blessings, large or small, look and feel insignificant. It insults
your significance. When envy's passion claims you, you are
left chasing someone else's life (whether it is realized or not)
while missing out on your own.

Do you have the courage to stay in your lane
and create value?

When we create value in our life, we open up more opportunity to love and serve. The challenge is envy is stuck trying to be someone else. Envy neglects all the value, potential, and resources. Can you delight in your life despite your apparent lack? For this reason, a discipline character reflects the right heart. Ultimately, discipline expresses a grateful heart that sees the rich blessings all around and can create opportunities for the future to explode.

Introduction

Lay down that terrible burden to always get your way.

RICHARD FOSTER, *CELEBRATION OF DISCIPLINE*

A farmer with forty years of experience lays down his crops. He plants them, waters them, and knows the seasons just right. He has gone through the process of planting and harvesting so many times, that he is hyper sensitive to the proper conditions to plant the right seeds and get the full harvest. He knows how much space to put between each seed. He knows how many seeds to plant and when is the best time to water them. He knows how deep to plant the seed.

As a child, he learned from his father, who was also a farmer. His father taught him how to work that soil. His father worked on farms for forty years. His father's father worked on farms, too. The knowledge they accumulated and passed down over the years was a bible of sorts of pure harvesting wisdom. They knew one thing however. That is, as Richard Foster so well puts it in his book Celebration of Discipline, "A farmer is helpless to grow grain; all he can do is provide the right conditions."

A farmer can do everything right to create the right environment to grow. But, to grow, the farmer needs to trust God. On one side, the farmer must be disciplined to make sure the seeds are planted with the right space to flourish and the right amount of water to grow.

On the other side, he must leave the growing part up to the Master Grower.

Discipline is the same way. You position yourself to unlock the best potential within yourself if you are planted in the soil. A seed cannot grow if it is never planted. It could not grow if it is never watered. It cannot grow if it is never in sunlight. That is, **you must take on proper disciplines to allow God to grow you**. On the other hand, the thing about the seed is, all its potential is tied to God. It is helpless to bring out its fruit without God.

Discipline allows you to place yourself before God.

Overview

When the Bible speaks of following Jesus, it is proclaiming a discipleship which will liberate mankind from all man-made dogmas, from every burden and oppression, from every anxiety and torture which afflicts the conscience... men escape from the hard yoke of their laws... we can only achieve perfect liberty and enjoy fellowship with Jesus when his command, his call to absolute discipleship, is appreciated in its entirety.

DIETRICH BONHOEFFER, PASTOR AND THEOLOGIAN IN GERMANY DURING WORLD WAR II

Located today in the Southwest of the UK, The Eden Project came about to house, as the Bible recounts, 'every plant that is pleasant to the eye and good for food.' The Eden Project is made up of multiple greenhouses called biomes. Each biome is shaped by an oval structure with hexagons patterning its surface.

The biomes include over one million different plants with waterfalls and boulders. It was completed in the year 2000. This place houses a rainforest.

Imagine you step into the greenhouse and walk through cleared pathways alongside dirt, plants, and the feeling of sunlight upon your face. As you explore the biome, the trail is covered with different types of ferns and flowers blooming from every side. It's a very interesting space.

Oddly enough, as you approach the west side of the biggest biome, you see a pile of dirt with no flowers, no leaves, no ferns growing. You wonder why it is empty. The entire place is flourishing, but it seems dead here.

Then, a volunteer begins to tell you that it seems the plants won't flourish here. With a spark of interest, you investigate. "What do you mean? Isn't this the same soil used for the other plants?"

"You're right," the volunteer says confidently. "The soil is the same soil I used for most of the plants in here... the only difference is the seeds I planted in that compartment would never stay in their place," he explained.

"What do you mean, they would never stay in their place?"

A bit puzzled by his flow of thought, you start wondering what he means by not stay in their place. Was it that they would sink to the bottom? Would children playfully move the seeds when the volunteers were not around? Curious, you begin to wonder why.

"The seeds don't stay in their place because I keep moving them," the volunteer says."It seemed they were not receptive to the environment near the wall that gave them extra sun. So, I put them in the center of the greenhouse where other plants would shade them during the day. But, they wouldn't grow there either. Later, I tried a mixture between the best of both worlds. Not too much shade, not too much sun. Sure enough, I thought they would begin to sprout. But, they didn't. It was like something was stopping them from growing. I checked the soil, the amount of moister in the ground, and even read an entire book to see if there was something a bit 'off.' Everything was satisfactory as far as I could tell.

It seems that the seeds we planted here won't keep alive because we move them too often.

Discipline is not the grueling parts of life, for the sake of misery and pain. Discipline is not for you to set goals that you cannot reach and fail and never try again. Discipline is not writing the same sentence 'I will not cheat on the test' fifty times for a teacher. Discipline is not depriving yourself of your favorite ice cream sundae.

Discipline is positioning. Just like humility, when a seed gets planted, it cannot be planted too deep in the soil and not to shallow, so is discipline to your life. Discipline is the positioning for a positive impact on others.

Our working definition for discipline in PBY is discipline **allows you to place yourself before God.**

Discipline Calls from Within Us

To the untrained, discipline is a taskmaster.

What is overlooked is that discipline is more than just an act itself. Specifically, discipline is not about checking a box every day or reading your Bible or waking up early in some attempt of self-righteousness or self-abasement.

Rather, the discipline of reading the Bible every day is placing it deep in your heart. It's about opening up time every day to allow God to speak to your life. Thus, Discipline is not legalism; though, they are often confused. God doesn't care much about the specific disciplines as what discipline calls from within us. And in due time, discipline calls from with us to bring out our very best potential.

Relationship (Not Requirement)

When a parent takes their child to a park, they will keep their child nearby. However, when a child is at school, the child can roam hundreds of yards away from the school staff and still be kept safe. That is, the school has fences (disciplines) that keep the child safe at a greater distance.

Strong adherence to discipline is a place of clarity. You have identified what you value, care about, and find worthy of your time. This framework gives us freedom in our relationship with God on what we do and how we do it. A train conductor who has to make an emergency stop (despite his scheduled arrival) because he sees something up ahead on the tracks needs the freedom within a framework to conduct his work. Otherwise, he is just a taskmaster.

People have distorted the value of discipline by viewing it as self-abasement. Self-abasement is rooted in guilt, shame, or vanity. Discipline is not the act of restriction for the sake of restriction. *Discipline is an act of guidance based on a relationship* (not a requirement).

Discipline builds a pure, undefiled relationship with God. Discipline is what makes recess fun. You get time to play and enjoy God's blessing in your life.

Created for Deep Work

When life beacons our attention at every moment (to recheck our email, scroll through our feed, or distract ourselves with some type of viewable media) we must be cautious of how these negative effects, caused by a world of distractions, could pose in reducing our space to have what Cal Newport calls deep work.

Deep work, as Newport defines, is the act focusing without distraction on a cognitively demanding task.

Discipline gives you the room to do what is most critical in your life, again and again. Discipline is what gives people value in a world of 'automate everything' and discipline gives people the power to make a way for the Kingdom when there is no way.

Deep work lets us create value. A quick question in a cognitively demanding task is not just a one-minute interruption. Now, one must re-engage in the material, find their place, focus their mind on the subject matter. It's like going into a deep cave for a hike. A quick question has a way of pulling you out in that instant. The challenge is that the only way to get back in is to trek the entire journey again. Plus, the more demanding the task, the more difficult it is to get back into it.

Discipline & Driving

Discipline is much like driving a car.

It deals with every aspect of driving and maintenance an average sedan demands.

For starters, everyone has one full tank of discipline each day. The better you set up your disciplines, the better mpg you will get from your tank. Imagine making a goal to get fit. If you have to spend time every day trying to decide what workout you should do, you will run yourself dry much quicker than if you already have a plan.

Instead, if you lay out your running essentials the night before, and you don't have to get up and pick out what you will wear, what you will eat, what you will listen to, you will use much less 'gas' from the tank. That means you have more energy to cover more miles in additional disciplines in other parts of your day.

It's much less about resisting every temptation as it is avoiding them all together. Exercising self-control is taxing when it comes to doing this in every area of your life. However, when you give yourself a plan, you use little to no gas to keep on track. The best part: just like a muscle you can train to grow, your discipline tank will grow with every day of training.

Discipline & Feeling

"Waiting for inspiration to write is like standing at the airport waiting for a train."

LEIGH MICHAELS, AUTHOR OF MORE THAN EIGHTY ROMANCE NOVELS.

Some days you will feel like being disciplined. The beginning of the year, around a significant holiday, or maybe around summer time. In either case, waiting for those days will guarantee you accomplish very little toward an actual discipline. Discipline can't be a roller coaster. That is too punishing. Discipline takes its best shape in small, incremental habits that lean on God to come to fruition. Discipline is a lifestyle.

Waiting for a better time won't work either. There often isn't a better time. The streetlights of life won't all turn green at the same time.

The key is not waiting for the perfect time (a.k.a feeling). There is no perfect feeling that will last through the hard times. Take small steps while using deadlines and accountability to shuffle through all the confusion and just do it. It is a powerful tool to know that other people are going to work with you toward your success.

Every Discipline Leads to Freedom

Discipline's value is found in the corresponding freedom. Every discipline has a corresponding freedom. It calls something from us and how we answer is important. Discipline works all the time, whether we do it intentionally or not. A discipline of poor eating leads to poor health the same way a discipline of smart budgeting leads to smart spending. You are the average of your top five checked and unchecked habits. Discipline is the surest way to position yourself for freedom.

Disciplines in Practice

Using the power of discipline you can live with less than you have, do what is vital over what is trivial, and make a big life that can love and serve radically out of small circumstances.

Discipline in practice is like the art of simplicity and meditation. Set your focus on God as your main resource above things and time. Disciplines like worship and prayer set your focus on God as your main source above worldly desires and the wrong heart.

Disciplines like submission give you the ability to give up your rights. It feels so good to give up your rights when you know you have a God who fights for you. Richard Foster said it like this, "Liberation comes from giving up your rights."

The discipline of finances, eating, and rest set your ability to live in moderation, a truly free state. The discipline of service to others puts God's people above yourself. Best of all, the discipline of joy will release you from a heavy yoke and refresh your spirit. Richard Foster said, "Of all people, we should be the most free, alive, and interesting."

A light heart is contagious.

These disciplines may not be pleasant in the moment, but they sure are worth it. The way to go is toward freedom.

Plus, as you improve one discipline, it makes it easier to improve another. For instance, if you start controlling your finances better and spending in moderation, you will be more equipped to do the same with your eating and time. One discipline is interlocked and influences the others—either in a positive or negative way.

The Value of Discipline

Start your day with your most ambitious goal.

Small, tiny steps every day are more important than one-off, large chunks of time. Discipline has a multiplier effect that compounds over time.

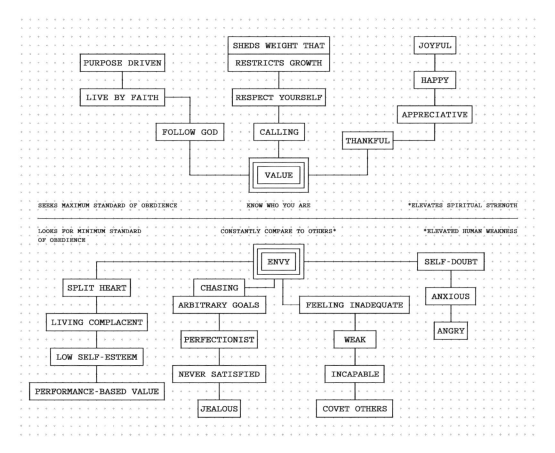

Two, plus two, plus two, plus another two, plus two does not equal ten. It equals 100,000.

Take the classic example: would you agree to have a penny today, that doubles for thirty days or $1 million right now? On day eighteen, the person who chose the penny only has $2,621. By day twenty-four, only six days later, the penny taker has $167,772. And by day twenty-seven, only three days later, the penny taker is now a millionaire with $1,342,177. Two plus two, plus two, plus two, plus two is not ten. It is 100,000.

Why do we not see this in discipline? Because very few people can hold good disciplines for extended periods of time.

In 2013 Warren Buffet averaged making $37 million a day. He did not make his first million when he was thirty. He was working quite diligently at business since the young age of thirteen. It took him thirty years to have a new worth of $1 million. It took him less than forty minutes, on average, to make that in 2013. Business Insider says, 99 percent of his wealth was made after his fiftieth birthday. *The power of building anything worth your lifetime may take a lifetime worth building.*

God is so ready to bless his children—but he cannot, at times—because we have left no room for him to reap. There is no soil tilled, no ground worked, and no quality to plant himself in and flourish. If you ask any investor or professional finance person, the best time to start, the answer will be... young. He just needs you to be planted and over time the value of discipline will be brought forth.

Discipline in Practice

Whatever He teaches us, He will give us the power to obey.

RICHARD FOSTER, THE CELEBRATION OF DISCIPLINE

Here is a simple outline of major disciplines in practice. Discipline is simply giving your life direction. With your specific practice, it will always take some adjustments to fit your preferences and styles.

Each of us can gain value from contrasting circumstances. You learn to be rich when poor, free when enslaved, content with ambitious, loving when hated, of measure in excess, and compassionate in deception, Jesus-like in daily commissary life, humble in prideful moments, listening when overlooked, simple and easy in busy and efficient, transparent and honest when influential, and confess when wrong, and forgiving even when you are right. Discipline brings power in revealing life in death.

Discipline is freedom in your everyday circumstances. Use this guide to develop a personal framework.

Much of our discussion here can be expanded in works like The Celebration of Discipline by Richard Foster.

1. **Discipline: Simplicity/Meditation**

    "Simplicity is freedom. Duplicity is bondage."
    RICHARD FOSTER

    1.1 Method: Imagine, you only needed 90% of what you currently have... is that possible? Most likely. Maybe you would get rid of some old clothes, a few books, and a couple things that you haven't touched since freshman year of high school. "Most of us," as Richard Foster put it, "could get rid of half our possessions without any serious sacrifice."

What about 70%? Can you live on just 70% of what you own? How about (this one will hurt) 30%? For every three things you have, get rid of two. And when it comes to future purchases, get only what is necessary and vital. What about a computer cleanse as well? We have stacks of files and programs and subscriptions that we may be able to do away with. Often we have things that make life more cluttered than valuable.

Do you need to buy that new _____? Know why you are purchasing something. Is it for purpose or pleasure? If you feel pressured to buy something, sleep on it. Or, if you must, see if there is a return policy. Always remind yourself that you have the room to breathe. On the flip side, it's fine to make purchases for pleasure. One must enjoy their earnings as well.

This also couples with meditation. The proper value of meditation is instrumental in giving us a life that is ours. When all hell breaks loose in our lives, mediation is immensely helpful. With that, we shouldn't wait for hell to practice this discipline. Focusing on God's word and feeding your mind with words that you write or say, begin to adjust your future today. Start your day with a healthy breakfast, then stretch. Use that time to stretch to focus on scripture or pray. Give God room to speak into your life. Ask God questions like how are you? How has heaven been? Do you need anything from me, today? All it takes is ten minutes. Spend that time in the car, music off, and on the way to work, praying. Take a 'pointless' walk with the sole aim to just focus on God. In other words, give yourself room from the worries of life.

1.2 Why: Living simply fights the urge to be greedy for gain. Your life focuses more on the quality of your life rather than the quantity. More will never satisfy a heart that needs only the essentials. And the key is this: Simplicity is not an outward lifestyle without an inward dealing.

1.3 Freedom: As Foster wrote, "Simplicity sets us free to receive the provision of God as a gift that is not ours to keep and can be freely shared with others." Simplicity eases your anxiety. In a world of increasingly more tools and toys, this discipline contends with all media and lifestyle demands. You become generous when you are 'simple' to fill. You are more full, more often, with less. Everything turns from an expectation to a gift. This discipline makes us better aware of kindness, openness, and simple love from others and toward others.

Meditation takes what life throws at us, and says I trust God. Refraining from compulsory reactionary workflow is a powerful tool that mediation could counter. You overcome the fear of being alone. You become ready to give yourself because you have been filled by good. You get deeper with God, trust in God, and are filled by God, just with a bit of meditation.

2. **Discipline: Fasting/Prayer**

We are no longer worried about how we could make ourselves more at peace, for we are attending to the impartation of peace within our hearts.
RICHARD FOSTER

2.1 Method: Set yourself up to pray and fast. These two things go hand in hand. When you fast, know that your stomach will yell and bicker, especially if you normally give it all it wants, all the time. Make it a point to fight through the small cravings for the larger appetite. Richard Foster suggests starting a fast from lunch to lunch. Fast even one meal a week, then over time, step it up to two meals, and possibly a whole day.

During this time, make your requests known to God. Pray for discernment. Offer up thanksgiving (show your gratitude). Pray for guidance. Speak. Listen.

Fasting increases your space to have time in prayer. At the same time, give Him who you are by unleashing who He is in you by simple undivided time in prayer. Prayer during a time of fasting is excellent as well. Approach God with a formally or informally. Give him thanks, for one thing, every morning. Mention something from the previous day. Mention something you are excited for that day.

Fasting could also be abstaining from a substance for twenty-one days. It could be coffee, chocolate, or movies. It could be your email. It could be anything that you are frequenting too much. Start slow and build. Make sure you are in control. Don't underestimate this power. Even if you are strict in discipline, the power of a twenty-one-day fast is always a good reminder of who is in control. Rest is the best remedy when you feel unable to continue the fast to completion.

2.2 Why: Fasting combats the mindset of poverty. A poverty mentality will cause people to feel a need to have another chocolate cookie, or another hour on the couch watching TV, as if they are running out. It says 'I don't have enough.' It implies that if I don't get my way, I will be ruined. It's our minds mechanism to protect us and avoid pain. This has been reinforced by past losses and being taught not to waste. Fasting, from food or anything in general, makes room for God to come in and gain control again.

2.3 Freedom: The art of this discipline comes not in the action itself, but in the posture of your heart that emerges. You show yourself more dependent on God. Plus, you become more honest with yourself. "We cover up what is inside us," Foster writes, "with food and other good things, but in fasting these things surface." What do you want to cover up with (it could be food, coffee, or an online network)?

Letting go of _____ by fasting shows us what controls us. It also opens a door for a new freedom we can acquire.

This discipline brings out our true selves. Fasting and prayer give us a sure way to monitor our hearts. It is much more difficult for the rich man—someone with excess food options, pleasures, and comforts to readily recognize their heart. Then, you will ask, is this all I was worried about losing?

Remember, prayer is not closed eyes and empty words. It is talking with God. It is a conversation with God. It is listening to God. Let me emphasize that last one; give God room to speak because it's easy to drown him out with problems and opinions and suggestions when he is ready and present with an answer. Today we struggle with listening more than ever before. A conversation is both speaking and listening.

3. **Discipline: Worship/Study**

To worship is to quicken the conscience by the holiness of God, to feed the mind with the truth of God, to purge the imagination by the beauty of God, to open the heart to the love of God, to devote the will to the purpose of God.
WILLIAM TEMPLE

3.1 Method: Study is the fundamental pursuit we learn from a three-year-old to ask the question why again and again. Study is different than meditation, as meditation is listening to someone you love and pondering over and over again about what they say. Study changes one's sequence of thinking. Study culture, your parent's history, their country of origin, the institutions which you are involved with. Google everything! And then Google it again. Study awards us to see how our actions, speech, and worldviews align to God's truth.

Specifically, when it comes to study, reading is incredibly valuable. Reading helps you uncover stories of success in areas that you may struggle with. When you get saved, your spirit is renewed immediately. Then after, your thinking needs to be renewed. Reading is one of the most valuable tools we have. It allows you to sit with some of the greatest minds in the comfort of your home. Our mind needs a shift for the power of God to be unleashed. I can look back at specific sentences or paragraphs in books that changed my life.

They say time for reading is only for the rich. Make your life rich by spending time in study.

In study, set out time each day to review scripture. It could be a book, the entire Bible in a year, or the study of one verse. When I first got saved, I committed to reading the Bible through the process of one year.

Worship can do much of the same thing. It has a way of refreshing the mind. It is something totally unorthodox to our natural tendency. Worship distinguishes one's heart stance toward the Father. Life is full of expectations and hopes and desires. When we can turn ourselves from our gain and lay it on Jesus, something magical happens. It's not about the quality of your voice, the particular song or the feeling you get while worshiping. It is about giving adoration and exaltation to Him. It's easy to get caught doing church activities and never giving him adoration. Worship is like good, appreciated design or art—you marvel at its beauty, praise its authenticity, and reflect on your understanding, all at the same time.

Keep worship fresh. When you go to a grocery store, the produce section is stocked with apples, bananas, and fresh grapes. Week after week, you go, and they have all the same fresh produce. Even though they have fruit every time, and the fruit looks the same, the fruit is fresh. Worship is the same way. Many church services begin with a worship set. That doesn't mean it's the same as last week. It's fresh every time. Letting go of last week's glory for this week's nutrition can demonstrate God's heart. Seek God afresh every time you worship, whether it is in a church service or a house.

When you worship and study, make it a point to get rid of your phone, turn off your computer, and give yourself to be distracted by Him alone.

3.2 Why: Both of these directly deal with your attitude. Study brings you in direct conflict with other ways of thinking. It challenges the way you choose to do things. It challenges the narrative you tell yourself. In the same way, worship pours our attention to God rather than ourselves. It opens room for breakthrough and insights. In light of that, both of these disciplines are valuable because they alter the way you look at the world around you. You learn how to give holy reverence to God through every aspect of your life.

3.3 Freedom: These disciplines as they are different in action, grant us some very similar qualities and freedom. Both give room for growth, understanding, feeling, and new convictions. How things relate in your world are built from how they relate in your mind. Study allows you to master your life, and worship allows you to remind your spirit what keeps you fresh.

4. **Discipline: Finances**

God has all the resources of the universe at His disposal. At the same time, He sees poor people who need to be fed, willing missionaries who need to be equipped and sent, and churches that need to be built. That's why His eyes are roaming Earth, looking for faithful-hearted stewards through whom He can channel millions of dollars into His Kingdom.
ROBERT MORRIS

4.1 Method: Being disciplined with our finances is a challenge. For instance, giving one-hundred dollars can be a big deal relative to circumstances. There are two pieces to finances: control and giving. Sometimes they contradict each other.

First, consider that your finances need to have some order. Start by making a priority list of what needs to get funded each month. Make sure that when you add items is on a need basis. Even if that means you must learn to live differently. Also, as young adults, saving for our future seems very distant. Savings simply creates breathing room in case of emergency.

This discipline alone can change the rest of your life. It can open your time to serve others.

Because this is a challenge, be honest with yourself. Don't hide where you are right now for some false optimism for the future. Confront the truth head on by having those difficult conversations with your parents, your employer, or your accountability (someone you trust).

Then, on the other hand, take what little you have and bless others. Don't go above your means, but be intentional to always be a blessing. Realize what you can do (and what you cannot do) and do that. Maybe you have a few extra dollars lying in your car for a homeless person you may see on your commute. Or, you can purchase a simple ten dollar book for a friend. Plus, some of the best giving is not money at all. Give your time, your energy, and your talents in charity to your local church.

The best time to start giving is not when you have a lot. Otherwise, a deferred giving plan is a heart stance that reads: I can only give out of my excess. Instead of that, give out of your surplus of generosity that God has blessed you with. God is looking for people he can trust to distribute funds through the Kingdom. He needs people who are responsible, wise, and ready to listen.

Don't overcomplicate giving. It all comes down to a heart issue and much less an amount issue.

Remember, the blessing is in giving. In this case, the results matter much less than the motive. It is easy to misinterpret our giving for an expectation of something in return. The less you expect, the more you will be surprised at what you gain. In The Blessed Life, Robert Morris speaks about his wife and him, "We found ourselves living more comfortably on 30% than we previously had on 90%."

When we have no expectation of anything in return, we realize the full power of giving. It's a powerful way to build trust with God and others just by initiating giving. Generosity is the heart of God. If God asks, listen. When God asks, listen. See what he will do. Also, see what he wants to do with your heart's intention.

4.2   Why: There are three major areas of our lives--finances, work, and relationships. When one is out of direction, especially finances, it can cause problems in the others. Marriages break because of bad financial order. When people are unemployed, mental stress builds a lot of pressure. Debt is something that can cause a lot of pain in every area of our life. Many people must make decisions from a place of financial obligation rather than Kingdom duty. That leaves little room for God to work. The discipline of finances releases a new world of blessing in your life.

4.3   Freedom: Giving confronts head on the fear of lack. You remind yourself every time you give (and don't know how you will supply the rest you need) that God is more than enough. And when money doesn't control you, you deal with your relationships better, you deal with your work better, and you can enjoy life much more.

5. **Discipline: Submission**

Lay down that terrible burden of always needing to get your way.
RICHARD FOSTER

5.1 Method: Submission is the willful decision to surrender humbly. It is complete self-denial in a moment or action or circumstance. God wants you at his disposal. That is only possible if you can forgo getting your way.

The discipline of submission confronts our ability to let go of our 'rightness.' Our rightness could be a smarter agenda or a more efficient tactic. However, submission is the act of saying nothing. Other times, it can be doing a task less efficiently. Submission allows you to realize your opinion is not as important as you think. You don't always have to say what is on your mind. Nor do you need to be super-efficient in everything you do.

A lot of times we get unsettled or frustrated when someone hinders our ability to be productive. The art of this discipline is when you are not easily frustrated when someone makes it harder for you to do your job. If a co-worker makes your assignment one day late, is it the death of you? Or, when a leader initiates a plan that you don't necessarily agree with, can you still give yourself fully to the job?

In that, it's much more important to have a submitted heart toward God than get your way, always be right, and justify yourself if someone misunderstands you. (Let them!) Do you need to prove yourself to be right? Do you need to test superfluously each and every word a pastor says from a pulpit, as if the Holy Spirit has granted him an unhuman ability to never get anything wrong? Don't major in the minors. Submission is done by willfully letting go of getting your way for a different way. That different way shines Kingdom values above personal agendas and tactics.

In the end, submit until the submission becomes destructive towards you. At that point, the submission is tyranny. Don't stand for what you shouldn't tolerate, but don't demand what you don't require to live a purposeful life.

5.2 Why: Always getting our way is a heavy burden to carry. Obviously, we shouldn't undermine our self-respect. Rather, we can let go of needing self-gratification in the name of self-respect.

Self-respect is the belief in your integrity and nothing more. When we demand self-respect to feel good about ourselves, we get in the way of releasing God's power. Demanding self-gratification is much different than demanding a certain respect from others. The key is never undermining your self-respect. Let me give you an example. Jesus ate with sinners and was ridiculed by the Pharisee's for it. He never allowed the Pharisees to undermine the authority of heaven. He kept his self-respect while he ate with sinners. Yet he never became a sinner.

When we submit, we put a higher value on what other people say and do. We are liberated to give up our way for a much greater purpose. Self-denial carries a spiritual authority and spiritual protection that is difficult to see. God covers those who are under his wing.

5.3 Freedom: The freedom that comes from giving up our rights internalizes a level of self-worth beyond respect, notoriety, or fame. Oddly enough, self-denial, as Richard Foster so powerfully points out, "is the only sure way to love ourselves." You are free to love others—whether you are winning or losing. This opens up a level of spiritual depth that is way too good to miss.

This is also the quickest path to leadership. Submission puts you in the best position to be molded, transformed, and shaped into your best design. "Frankly, most things in life," Foster points out, "are not nearly as important as we think they are. Our lives will not come to an end if this or that does not happen."

6. Discipline: Service

No one wanted to be considered the least. Then Jesus took a towel and a basin and redefined greatness.
RICHARD FOSTER

6.1 Method: The discipline of service is a lifestyle, not a one-week journey. Tony Robbins says it best: "Learn to do more for people, than anyone else." Service is, in essence, availability. And availability means vulnerability. Make yourself free to give of yourself. To give yourself—either your time, energy, ability, connections, and resources.

How can you better serve the community of people around you? Think through your opportunity to serve in your home, work, school, and church. What are the organization goals? Can I help clean something, build something, buy something, or give something? How can I surprise them? How can I create smiles on their faces? How can I shine God's light on them? Then do that. The power of service comes in action, not intention.

Another form of service is listening. People who can listen have a wide display of likable characteristics. When you are a good listener, people will walk away and say "that person is awesome." They might not even learn much about you. They just feel free to share themselves with you. That is a very powerful form of service.

6.2 Why: This is the most direct life-giving thing you can do. The world puts a crushing weight on us. Service is a free act you can do to help release that burden on others. Give yourself an immensely valuable trait by opening your eyes and spirit to how you can serve others at any moment.

6.3 Freedom: The freedom of service is peace in the moment and peace in your schedule. When things are delayed, you resound with an overwhelming sound of calmness. You give Jesus control over your time. We are often worried about wasting time. Service will kill the fear of unproductivity swiftly.

7. **Discipline: Time**

How did it get so late so soon?
DR. SEUSS

7.1 Method: None of the disciplines mean anything without time. Time gives discipline the place to grow and flourish. In also unlocks what Darren Hardy calls big 'Mo.' Big Mo is the momentum of consistency. It is what financial advisors call the power of compounding. Time is one of your most important assets, especially because you are young.

When your priorities meet your time, that is where genuine living happens. Lift your values and standards by setting order to your time. Many successful people have a morning routine. They workout, read something inspiring, or spend time with their family. In any case, there are things you can do every day that are small, simple tasks that open the door to the power of this discipline.

Our time is a precious commodity. Time wasted is most peoples' biggest regret. And, most people look back on their lives and wish they had embraced the moment more. Make it a point to do it now.

Begin by defining two or three simple routines you want to live by. Identify them, write them, and begin. The value of reading your Bible every day is not that every day you get incredible insight. Rather, it is that you open yourself to interact with God and potentially gain valuable insight. There is a distinction. Creating that space is important. It allows your brain to enter into that space and be free.

7.2 Why: Time is something we too easily give away cheaply and something that is most valuable to us. Our time is the most important piece we have in bringing our purpose to reality. God gives you the time you need to work your purpose. Your obligation is to allocate that time accordingly.

7.3 Freedom: When you organize your day, you no longer are slave to busyness for the sake of busyness. The freedom here comes in a prized set of priorities that allows you to give yourself the proper space to think/do/learn. When you decide what you will do with your time, you decide what you will do with your life. That gives you the freedom to enjoy it and walk in it.

Finally, and most importantly, practice the discipline of joy and celebration. Richard Foster said, "Of all people, we should be the most free, alive, and interesting." Joy and celebration is one aspect of our life too many forget and overlook. Don't be so dignified that you lose sight of breaking out. Dance. Sing. Shout. Laugh loud. Make it a point to be free. You have too much good stuff ahead to be a stiff young adult. Just think, those old people who are stiff were probably stiff when they were young. Have fun, enjoy this life. It's too good to let joy just pass us by.

The best part of all of this, as you begin, it only gets easier. The challenge is then beginning. Or, in another perspective, the challenge is ending a chaotic way of life for a more essential, minimal, quality way of life. Discipline builds the space required to anticipate danger and mishap while giving you the ability to maximize any opportunity for the highest return.

Isn't that a big part of what it means to be a disciple? Jesus said to go and preach the gospel, right? But to do that, we need the freedom from our home, food, dependency on work and 401k plans. We need the freedom to go when he calls us to go.

Note: Take appropriate measures to develop in each discipline, as there are always more disciplines you can develop into your daily life. There is always room to grow, so do not force too much pressure at once.

Culture Asks

To be yourself in a world that is constantly trying to make you something else is the greatest accomplishment.

RALPH WALDO EMERSON, AMERICAN ESSAYIST

In Palo Alto, California, it was a Sunday morning in August. Police cars drove around town collecting students who were involved in criminal activity. The students were picked up from their homes, brought to the station to be fingerprinted, read their Miranda rights, and fully booked. Their cell was not located at the police station, however. They were located in the downstairs basement of the Stanford University psychology building.

The students had agreed to be a part of an experiment. As they arrived, they were blindfolded and set in a prison cell. The basement was turned into a fully transposed prison chamber for the experiment. They had no idea that they were at Stanford University.

The proposed time was set out to last for two weeks. Philip Zimbardo, a psychologist at Stanford University, found participants by putting an advertisement in the paper that read, "...Psychology study of prison life. $15 a day for 1–2 weeks beginning Aug. 14." The participants were divided in half, by flipping a coin. Half became the guards; the other half became prisoners.

This experiment was conducted to learn about why prisons are such nasty places. The prisoners were taken in, stripped down, searched, and sprayed down to make sure they were not bringing any germs into the facility. A huge state of humiliation. Each prison inmate was given a number and no longer referred to by name.

On the first night, at two in the morning, the guards blasted a whistle to wake up the prisoners and ordered them to do push-ups. The next day, the prisoners ripped off their numbers in an act of self-value, and they barricaded themselves in their cells.

The guards were instructed to keep the prisoners in line. They worked on three different eight-hour shifts to keep the prisoners fully occupied. They were given no specific training on this. Yet their response was, "The guards broke into each cell, stripped the prisoners naked, took the beds out, forced the ringleaders of the prisoner rebellion into solitary confinement, and generally began to harass and intimidate the prisoners."

Every aspect of the prisoners' lives fell under the complete control of the guards on duty—even when they were allowed to go to the bathroom. This gave the prisoners a mental shaking. So much so, the first prisoner was dealing with a lack of clarity, rage, crying, and emotional instability. When they found out that he was really in a state of suffering, only thirty-six hours into the experiment, he was released.

Over time, the prisoners tried to create an escape plan. This only led to further humiliation and harsh treatment from the guards. The plan never came about. They were forced to do more push-ups, jumping jacks, and even clean the toilet bowls with their bare hands.

Later in the experiment, more than half the prisoners sat down with a chaplain. When they introduced themselves to him, they used their number instead of their name.

After countless events, the prison experiment that was to last two weeks had to be terminated on the sixth day. The state of the prisoners and the abuse of the guards had gone too far.

After the experiment, one prisoner said, "I realize now that no matter how together I thought I was inside my head, my prisoner behavior was often less under my control than I realized."

When it comes to discipline, our actions make or break us. Undoubtedly, our environment plays a very large role in what disciplines we value.

Camp Life

In modern society, many people can live in a state of a luxurious slave camp. Specifically, many people will focus on a bigger income, lifestyle goals, and fitting into the crowd. What we can realize is how our circumstances can influence our identity, goals, and decisions.

One of the prisoners in the Stanford experiment said, "I began to feel that that identity, the person that I was that had decided to go to prison was distant from me—was remote until finally, I wasn't that, I was 416. I was really my number."

Recall that the two-week experiment got cut short. That each prisoner willfully signed up and knew it was only going to end. Nevertheless, the circumstances they found themselves in had an overpowering influence over them.

Maybe you find yourself in a set of circumstances that you did not plan. Part of discipline is staying in your lane. Yet, another key part is paving your lane.

Your actions are heavily influenced by the world around you. Most people live in a spiritual imprisonment. It doesn't matter if you have nice clothes or drive a nice car. 'Camp life' is a simple state of internal imprisonment despite vocation, position, location, or circumstance. You can be in an impoverished nation or a prosperous nation, and camp life can have an adverse effect on you.

Think of cliché's like 'time is money' or 'work hard, play hard.'

If time is money, then we have a big problem. You will never be content.

Work hard and play hard is only valid if you are living with direction. God makes it clear to focus on purpose before setting your site on specific projects. If not, we can do a million things for God and never actually be with God.

In the same fashion, your neighborhood, your school, and your friends have the power to influence your decision making.

A true prisoner, Viktor Frankl, said, after being imprisoned in Auschwitz during World War II, "The human being is completely and unavoidably influenced by his surroundings." For Viktor, his surroundings become a prison. He was subjected to a real camp life and the SS guards and the tiny bit of soup each day.

The forces Viktor experienced were obvious. For many, the forces that influence our decisions are less obvious. For instance, there was a study done where participants who held warm coffee or iced coffee, were asked to describe a person they knew or had just met.

Their response was bent toward describing the person relative to the temperature of the liquid in their cup. If they held a hot cup of coffee, they described the person as warm. On the other hand, people who held the iced coffee, described the person as cold. Our mind has an unconscious ability that draws it towards what it has last experienced.

The things that happen to you yesterday have a larger effect on you then what you made as a resolution for the new year one month ago. Can you remember your struggles from this day last year? Probably not. Yet, most of our decisions are influenced by what is happening right around us.

Major life goals can have a large benefit for you and your future, and you could have more resolve and passion about bringing forth these goals, but there is something about yesterday's argument, lack of discipline, sin or failure has the power to creep into our minds much louder. I start my writing every day by saying, "This is bigger than me and my week. This is bigger than *yesterday*."

Viktor went on to say, "When we are no longer able to change a situation—we are challenged to change ourselves." In light of this, the power of context tells us that even with any external factors, one has the power to position themselves in a fruitful position before God.

Discipline

Challenger: Envy

Discipline never seeks to destroy life but to foster, strengthen, and heal it!

RICHARD FOSTER, *CELEBRATION OF DISCIPLINE*

Imagine I sent you off on a journey to Thailand, a beautiful country in the heart of Southeast Asia. Upon your departure, I gave you about $100,000 in Baht (THB), Thai currency (nearly THB3,500,000).

In Thailand, that will buy you lots of things. You would live like a king! Rent is a quarter of the price compared to some parts of New York or California.

Then, after six months in Thailand, you decide to travel to Europe.

There you locate a place to stay for the next three months. You have enough money from your time in Thailand to afford a furnished home. You pay the leasing party more first-month rent and deposit.

They look at you odd and say, we don't accept this, we only accept Euros.

Nonetheless, there are three things to remember. The currency still possesses potential value. The currency is real. The currency is yours. The only difference: the currency's worth doesn't have the same buying power.

Envy works the same way when we take what value we are given and try and use it in a 'world' that is not our domain to achieve some arbitrary goal. That arbitrary goal could be a certain lifestyle, bank account, or position. It will be a never-ending tug-a-war with the world for value. A negative distraction that misguides, misjudges, and misinterprets our true value.

The hardest truth about envy—when we are jealous of what other people have to the point we chase after it—is that envy reveals that you struggle to appreciate your value.

Where Did All My Value Go?

Envy has this thing with value: it miscalculates the value of what you have in comparison to what another has. Envy never reminds you that you came from humble beginnings nor that everything you have is a gift.

Envy is never satisfied. This is different than passion because envy is like a vacuum and passion is like a quench. The difference is subtle but think of it this way. A great athlete will be passionate for the next win, by doing his best every game. An envious sportsman will be driven for the next win, by doing his best in every game. The difference is that the envious player will not be satisfied with the win. They will constantly be searching for another win.

This leads to low-quality thinking and character. Value is misjudged. Looks, position, vocation, and talent become the sum total of who you are. And, the answer never suffices.

Can you delight in your disparity?

In essence, one lives a life of performance-based identity (that will never win) to elevate human weakness, rather than discovering her true kingdom ability. One gets stuck comparing lifestyle accomplishments to others rather than comparing oneself against oneself for the betterment of character.

Envy Towards Us

Envy comes from people with higher authority, from our friends, and people who have accomplished little.

First, envy can come from authority figures by age or position.

David was anointed to be King before he did anything worthy of being king. When David said I will fight Goliath, he immediately had haters. Particularly, his eldest brother, Eliab, was most envious. Eliab was envious of his courage.

Envy revealed itself three times. After David had said I want to go against Goliath, Eliab made these remarks.

First, in an attempt to show responsibility: "With whom have you left those few sheep?" Eliab asked. I don't think he was worried about what was happening with the sheep. Then, Eliab's hidden agenda came out: "I know your presumption and the evil of your heart," he continued. The evil of your heart? To fight Goliath? What did he think David was trying to do? Fight Goliath and fail so Israel would fall? That's a big risk because the only way for that to play out would be for David to get killed, and I don't think Eliab would want that. Then, in a final attempt of explanation, his personal insecurity came out, "Why have you come down?"

When authority comes from others, it's like crabs in a barrel. Feeding the envy or listening to the envy only leads to more envy.

Your future is too important for the short-term satisfaction of an envious heart.

How Does This Change Your Life?

It was character that got us out of bed, commitment that moved us into action, and discipline that enabled us to follow through.

ZIG ZIGLAR, AMERICAN AUTHOR

At Apple, the directly responsible individual (DRI) system is used to make clear who the responsible individual will be for a project. DRIs are accountable to the team, company, and customers. Being the DRI makes it hard to have excuses.

This also eliminates deferred responsibility.

In a real life example, on March 13, 1964, Catherine Genovese was returning home from work around 3:00a.m.. As she approached her apartment, she was attached and stabbed by a man. She lived in an apartment building in New York. Dozens of people heard her screaming. Famously put into text by Malcolm Gladwell, thirty-eight people to be exact. The first attack began at 3:20a.m., and the first call to the police happened at 3:50a.m.. Why did it take so long for anyone to respond?

When 37 other people could have called the police, it's easy to defer the responsibility to someone else.

This story reveals a telling truth (something Apple counters with DRI) that has been confirmed in multiple studies. Deferred Responsibility or 'Bystander Apathy' happens when we don't feel responsible.

When it comes to our lives, it's easy to do the same thing. When we find ourselves in the middle of life, it's easy to not feel responsible for our circumstances. Discipline is when you decide to take responsibility.

I would never follow a leader who defers responsibility. I wouldn't want a bus driver, an airplane pilot, or a doctor to do the same.

How do you change bystander apathy, in your own life? Disciple. Stop making excuses and confront the brutal facts of your situation. Discipline is the autonomy (freedom) and framework needed to accomplish a given task that is set on your life, responsible for making it yours, and ready to cut everything that gets in the way of that. These are not rules. Rules are in place for disobedience. Discipline is in place for a lifestyle of rapid obedience.

Discipline Is Always Useful

I know what my most important task is today. It is writing my book. Most everything else is trivial. Despite that clear knowledge, my mind will drift and focus on others things.

I wonder if I could eliminate even 40 percent of the trivial things in my life, how much more clarity and calmness of thought I would have. I believe this is why simplicity starts within the mind, not the daily task list.

Things seem pressing, like the newest email, the newest text message, the newest video, the newest problem. Plus, today we have more ways to store stuff to come back to later. Bookmark that page, 'watch later,' save, screenshot, add to, etc. We have much more information today that we can review and dissect than ever before. Discipline will change your life when you decide to have focus and a framework in a world of distraction and ambiguity.

Trivial tasks—disguised under time management skills—is something we must confront today much more. Time management, in all its hooray and hurrah, needs to be vetted for one key element, usefulness.

Peter Drucker, a management icon said, "There is nothing quite so useless, as doing with great efficiency, something that should not be done at all."

What Drucker is revealing, and what we must consider in a character that is instructed to be disciplined (planted), is that most likely 80 percent of what we did yesterday was trivial. If we are realistic, 98 percent of what we do is trivial. In light of Kingdom values, what you manage to do with your time can be world changing.

Discipline reflects that you know how to say yes to your lane and no to everything outside your lane. You identify the few, essential things that are important to your success and eliminate the others.

Cut Out the Trash

With so much knowledge and information and people and things and options and opportunities and resources, discipline teaches you to cut out the trash. If more knowledge or information or people or things or options or opportunities or resources were the answer, we would all be Buffet rich, with an Island, and eat only lobster tails (because lobster tails are amazing)!

Don't fool yourself. More knowledge or another degree are seldom what you need. Action is. Discipline yourself in what they taught you as a child—not to lie, to share, to be kind, to show respect. It's amazing how adults struggle with the things they taught us as children.

You take in sixteen hours a day of stuff, make it top quality.

Greatness Redefined

The idea of greatness refers to anything that is increasing in size. What we typically associate with greatness—title, wealth, or position—all resemble an exterior expansion. As if, what is on the outside comes first. Quite often this leads to some challenges. We would assume all presidents, kings, and queens would have a rightful spot in heaven by the nature of their position. Or, the one hundred wealthiest people on the planet would be seated at the right hand of Jesus. As it is, title, wealth, or position are effervescent in nature. They fizzle up and foam out. Discipline unlocks true greatness by redefining it toward ultimate (internal) freedom rather than external attainment.

This type of mental shift will free you up to make better decisions. Rather than contemplating what job to take or what city to live in or what school to go to, you contemplate what gives you the highest internal freedom. Much of our struggle with decision-making is based on the opportunity cost. Losing money or resources or something. If you identify what internal freedom you will gain, I assure you, this mindset will have a positive expansion in your life.

To be the best version of you—everything God created you to be, to go from good to great, your life lies in the disciple to cultivate your unique lane. It takes discipline to say no to the opportunity that does not align with your lane. It takes discipline to live intentionally and leverage your resources toward maximum capacity.

With this in mind, don't disregard the opportunities in front of you (the things you are involved with today) for the success you are searching for—whether big or small. Sometimes, to get to where you want to go, you have to deal with where you are.

Give your security to Jesus, not the 3P's. If that means walking in absolute insecurity, it is worth it.

A Full Tank

Imagine that you end up in the desert in a car. You drive around aimlessly because you cannot find the main road. You want to get back to civilization. As you drive through the day, you grow more and more anxious because you have limited gas and water and don't want to get stuck. The night is coming, you do not see a road, and you are nearly out of gas. Frustrated and tired, you fall asleep.

The next day, you wake up, and you look to find that your gas tank has been refilled and your water supply replenished. This happens each day. As you realize that some magical thing is doing this, you realize you can take a more strategic approach to trying to find civilization. You begin to strategize which way to drive and what you will do. You are not sure of where you are going, but you are sure of what you want to accomplish in yourself.

That is discipline. Where would you drive, if every morning, you had a full tank? Call it $37 million. Call it a business that employees hundreds of people. Call it a hospital that cares for hundreds of patients. Whatever your passion, whatever your drive, your purpose calls you to discipline yourself to use that limited lot each day, rightfully, dutifully, and with a clear intention to elevate the Kingdom.

When to Start

Is it too late to start? Hershey's Chocolate was started by an orphan, well thirty-seven-year-old Milton Hershey. Gordon Moore began Intel at the quaint age of thirty-nine and Amancio Ortega Gaona, now one of the richest people in the world, started Inditex fashion group, known for Zara chain stores, at age thirty-nine1.

Is it too late to start? No.

When should you start? Now.

Larry Page started Google at twenty-five, Phil Knight started Nike at age twenty-six, John Mackey started Whole Foods at age twenty-seven, and Dee Hock started Visa at age twenty-nine.

What can you begin today?

How we spend our days is, of course,

how we spend our lives.

Annie Dillard

He disciplines us for our good, so that we may share His holiness. For the time being no discipline brings joy, but seems sad and painful; yet to those who have been trained by it, afterwards it yields the peaceful fruit of righteousness [right standing with God and a lifestyle and attitude that seeks conformity to God's will and purpose].

Hebrews 12 (AMP)

Discipline

Go! Guide

This section below will equip you with proper mindsets around discipline.
Don't forget there is additional material at purposebuiltyoung.com/resources.

Knowledge is not power. Action is. Execution trumps knowledge, every day of the week.

TONY ROBBINS, ENTREPRENEUR, BEST-SELLING AUTHOR, AND PHILANTHROPIST

Sculpting Takes Time

Michelangelo carved his first marble sculptor at the age of twenty-five. He called it Pieta, meaning 'pity or compassion.' The work depicts Jesus, after the crucifixion, in the hands of Mary. This was a special piece of work for Michelangelo.

Michelangelo had a lot of up and down emotions in his career. He had a lot of doubt. Despite that, looking back now, we know that he will be known throughout history. That is because he made Pieta, he was able to make the David, a sculpture that stands in Italy as a centerpiece for the rest of time. There would be no David without Pieta.

The thing is, discipline is built in the same way marble is carved, overtime. You build, and build, and build, despite a down emotion or an up emotion.

The Gorilla Right in Front of Us

When you execute on an idea, you cannot overlook your day's value for next year's potential. That is a bad allocation of resources. That is like trekking around the world and only focusing on the final destination.

Execute your daily activities with excellence and make sure you are accomplishing your plans and objectives—no matter how chaotic your life is. The best creatives understand that to do deep work, they must eliminate disorder to the best of their ability.

We spend most of our lives dealing with the plans and activities right in front of us, ticking tasks off our list, clicking past mile markers on our biggest projects, responding to the incessant demands on our time. And we can easily miss the gorilla right in front of us.

JIM COLLINS

Daily Reading

Read your goals daily. When you begin to read your goals daily, you internalize them. It's the same reason way reading your Bible every day is critical. Over time, you will either relate more to the goals or feel the goals were not relevant to you. It helps you to reflect your reality on your goals. It's easy to make our life goals something other people will be able to admire. Rather, make them something you will admire. Read them daily by placing them on your phone, on your desk, on your wall, in your bathroom, or even in your Bible. Anywhere you can read them every single day.

Taking Simple Steps

If you want to be an awesome writer, write every day. If you want to be an awesome teacher, teach every day. Regardless if you have an audience or not. If Michelangelo waited for world class fame to show up, we would never have seen any of his works.

You can be the most talented or dumbest person, that doesn't matter. The truth is, as Darren Hardy so well outlines in his book The Compound Effect, "What's most interesting about this process to me is that, even though the results are massive, the steps, in the moment, don't feel significant."

Writing for an hour a day doesn't seem so glamorous. The winds of creativity don't come rushing in every day. It's unlikely that you will see them every week. What's more important, though, is not the actual results as what consistency does in and through you.

Set up small, simple steps you can do every day that would be insignificant by themselves, but when done consistently, hold the potential to change your future. Big ideas are easy. Buying new domains is fun. Executing one idea, giving it a position and coding a website, now that's hard.

As Thomas Edison once said, "Genius is 1% idea and 99% perspiration."

You are equipped to do what you need to do. To authenticate your journey and clear a path for others to begin their own, you make the small, seemingly insignificant choice every day to do, to be, to go, to walk, to run, to eat healthy, to read, to pray, to worship, to make, to create. What small steps can you start today to set your future in the course you believe (by faith) God is taking you?

At the beginning of your day: What is one thing you can do today to get closer to your goal? Make it your top priority (and complete it no matter what). In one year, you won't see much of change. In two years, you won't see that much more. But, in three years or four years, the results are clear.

Experiment

When Edison tried to create the light bulb, he did not fail 1,000 times, he experimented. When Paul addressed church leaders, he experimented. His letters were experiments.

What is an experiment? A procedure to make a discovery, test a hypothesis, or demonstrate a known fact.

Our entire journey is an experiment.

No one knows what will work and what will be successful. Even the best formulas for story and life don't immediately create wealth. To create, you experiment. Therefore, you must experiment to create.

In your life, will this new, uncontrollable external variable (a lack of resources, a break-up, a poor job situation) dictate your ability to create? What constrictions are holding you back from experimenting?

Your walk with God is just that: a walk with God. A relationship. You need to experiment. There is nothing normal about faith. If you are unsure of something or why you should believe something, ask about it, learn about it, buy books on it, talk to God about it, and do what you need to test it.

Organized Capture

Watch what God does. He moves all the time. This is one of my favorite parts of life. Organized Capture is the practice of always being ready to take in what God is telling you. You will experience revelations throughout your day. Have a place where you can jot your notes. Where you can recount the experiences where you saw God show up and the ideas he gave you. Use your phone and make different pages of notes that document subjects like my future, my current challenges, God's heart, and whatever you feel God is doing in your season. By revelation, I mean any insight God gives you into your life, the people around you, and your future.

Organized capture is leveraging the power of technology to overcome our short attention spans and memories. God gives us revelations every day that are big in power and easy to forget. We need a way to capture and review them.

Yes, you can re-listen to the podcast, but it's much harder to recreate moments. God gives you revelation while you are driving (thank God for Siri).

For me, a lot of ideas stir (sometimes the best ideas) while I am away from my pen or laptop. I probably get about ten to fifteen revelations a day. They happen when I am in conversation or when I am ordering a coffee. Trying to remember all of them would make me go crazy!

Organized capture is the practice of having pre-organized locations to capture life-giving thoughts for proper utilization. Don't let your dreams stay in your head. Write them. Record them. Revisit them. They often help build your faith. I simply use the notes section of my phone. It could be as elaborate as you like or as simple. The main thing is quick accessibility.

All Dressed Up and Nowhere to Go

Discipline, when you start, feels like a chore. It's like dressing like a CEO when you are a junior in the company. Don't do this because this is the standard. Do it because it is your expectation on yourself. Value yourself more than what the world has defined you as.

None of this is magic. It is so simple that it is easy to not do. You need to get in the habit of doing the seemingly insignificant tasks every day. Then, and only then, you begin to maximize your potential amidst the status quo of what life has served you. Dress the part, even if you don't have the part yet. This, my friend, makes life much more intriguing.

Be a Learner

Lifelong learning is something the current economy is asking from us. It is totally new from the old mentality of going to college, then working for forty years. Yet, this was always God's plan. He said mediate on my precepts (my commands) day and night.

When you position yourself this way, even when people are repeating information you may have heard before, you learn.

When you identify a trait that needs work, never forget that you can always grow daily. Maybe you get mindless tasks from your boss. You control your response 100 percent. What do you do? You humble yourself and do what needs to be done. In the same way, you get a large promotion at work. What do you do? You humble yourself and are now able to serve a bigger sphere of influence at the company. It will demand more, so you must also be more disciplined.

Create Your Schedule, Create Your Journey

While listening to interviews from successful people, each of them carried this very detailed, almost over-the-top meticulous schedule for their mornings. I wake up at 4:14 every morning. I drink a power smoothie for breakfast after my exercise. I read something inspirational for thirty minutes exactly. I shower while my coffee is brewing. I don't check my email until after 10a.m. I spend thirty minutes deciding what I want to do with my day before I start. Some of the details would seem so unnecessary, if they didn't have a resolve to create. Creating a life of your dreams calls for being purposeful about your entire life. It's not a special gene either. It is simply showing up. Every day.

CTRL + Z

I can click two buttons and take back what I just did. I can do it again and again. You cannot do that with your future. You cannot do it with your youth. Enjoy it. Don't set it up for a CTRL+Z back-up plan.

Those never work. You can never undo your school years, your debt, or your youth. This is not to scare you. Rather open your eyes to the reality that you are alive and able to reinvent and pioneer your life, today.

Most Important Task

My most important task today is:

→ _____

Most everything else is trivial.
Don't let my mind drift and wander.
I will thrive by completing this task today.

Your greatest story is now on the other side of what you build within internal sovereignty.

You answered the call. You have identified the variables within the Social Terrain and setbacks. You are aware of your story and what that means in the grand narrative of the world. You are building character—a quality that God wants in you. Now it is time for you build the quality that prizes God's grand design in your life.

> "Therefore, brothers and sisters, be eager to confirm your call and election. Do this and you will never ever be lost."

2 PETER COMMON ENGLISH BIBLE (CEB)

You know are equipped to overcome the challenge against suffering, doubt, and envy. You are not confused about what is most important in your life. Keeping a humble spirit, having faith, and fighting for discipline is a daily practice.

Now... what? What will your future measure up to?

Sir John Templeton, a modern version of humanity's best self, was able to look at the most difficult situations in the world and help improve them for the greater good. Sir Templeton passed away in 2008, and by that time had given away one of the most charitable gifts ever—over $1 billion. A man who integrated every aspect of his life in relation to his spiritual life said, "I'm a student always trying to learn. I am a sinner, all of us are. I've tried to be better day by day. Particularly, I try to keep asking myself what are the purposes of God? Why did God create the universe? What does God expect of his children here? And the closest you can come, in a few words, is He expects us to grow spiritually."

Your spiritual growth will naturally call you to pioneer your future.

That is part of the design our Father gave us. We all have a person-specific call to answer, and that means we don't have any other option but to pioneer.

3

Your Future

Your Future

All things are possible… for one who believes

JESUS, MARK 9

When you begin to bring forth an intentional lifestyle, your future becomes whatever you want it to be. What you soon realize is the challenge of affirming your calling and purpose every day is believing in yourself. You become your own worst enemy. If you don't believe in yourself, no one will. Mindset has much to do with your future.

Plus, the greater the challenge, the more it will be emphasized just how exceptional the qualities you will need to display to reach your final goal. Life will ask for more from you. It will present opportunities and moments that will test your confidence.

The first thing to determine your future will be your ability to believe in yourself.

To believe in your calling, everything inside of you will be tested.

Your future will require you to be accountable to yourself and others. To never settle toward apathy or complacency. These tests combine to present a woman or man worthy of their calling. The journey will present many failures but over time, your call will present itself with a higher and higher level of clarity that will be more and more difficult to attain. Nevertheless, we are to persevere.

This is the life of a pioneer. The pioneer will see exactly what they have to do and do it.

Life Constriction 3: Arrival and Frustration

The best way to predict the future is to invent it.

ABRAHAM LINCOLN, FOUGHT FOR THE ABOLISHMENT OF SLAVERY DURING A TIME WHEN SLAVERY WAS COMMONPLACE

Sometimes, in the middle of our best seasons, unexpected challenges will arise. Life has a way of throwing very turbulent moments at us. For me, I seem to fail the hardest when I am growing the most. When I hit a new level of capacity and achievement, I am most susceptible to fail. And fail hard. The challenge will seem impossible to overcome. But, the way to continue to progress toward what life asks from us is to out beat our current best (whether it be in work, health, discipline). To face a new challenge, bigger than anything you have ever faced before, we must pioneer.

If the core of our challenge is believing in ourselves, the darkest moments we face come when we give up on ourselves.

At times, as we steadily move forward, the battle gets rough. The terrain gets harsh. What happens to us then, just like the disciples on the boat with Jesus, is all too important. It is where our hopes intersect with reality. It is where our faith is put to the test. It is where our best selves are created.

When we no longer want to believe in our dreams. We feel like we are incapable. When everything is telling us to quit, the pain is unbearable, and life is at the last straw. At that point, we know a breakthrough is close.

Apathy and Complacency

Life shrinks or expands in proportion to one's courage.

ANAÏS NIN, ESSAYIST

Two people could go through the same situation and both come out different. Why? Because *how* they walked in.

In psychology, someone with a high *internal* locus of control (LOC) believes in their ability to control events affecting them. They attribute the outcomes of life events to something devised by their own control. They don't look for luck or toward the difficulty of a task to define their ability. They believe they are capable. In other words, they are a *bona fide* pioneer.

Someone with a high *external* LOC attributes chance and luck to life events. Some remedial, outside force, whether it be God or coincidence, has aligned something in their favor. When difficult tasks come, they are subdued. Life just seems to happen to them.

One person can have a high internal LOC, and another have a high external LOC and walk into the same situation, and come out with different outcomes. What they *believe* about themselves walking in is what makes the difference.

Especially when you are young, what you believe about yourself matters. When no one sees your value or understands your worth, do you have the courage to bring your best self into existence?

There is no path for you unless you create it.

To pioneer, you must believe. That is the only way you can even begin to outbeat your current best. Otherwise, you will become apathetic and complacent.

Life will ask you if you have the courage to chart your own journey?

Introduction

I don't believe in people just hoping. We work for what we want. I always say that one has no right to hope without endeavor, so we work

AUNG SAN SUU KYI, POLITICIAN AND OPPOSITION LEADER OF MYANMAR

After Jackie Robinson had joined the major leagues as the first black player, the world shifted. As a devote Christian, what Jackie Robinson set out to do was not be the best at baseball. He was charged with a much higher calling: to pioneer his journey.

Robinson would have to deal with, as Eric Metaxas retells in *Seven Men*, "On the road, hotels and restaurants refused service to Jackie, forcing him to eat and sleep away from the team. Letters arrived, containing death threats. Players on other teams kicked Jackie, stepped on his feet, struck him on the head with pitches, and even slashed painfully at his leg with their spikes, one time creating a seven-inch gash in his leg. Despite all of it, Jackie kept his cool."

At 28-years-old, Jackie Robinson got signed to the Brooklyn Dodgers.

After Jackie Robinson had joined the major leagues as the first black player, the world shifted. As a devote Christian, what Jackie Robinson set out to do was not be the best at baseball. He was charged with a much higher calling: to pioneer his journey.

Robinson would have to deal with, as Eric Metaxas retells in *Seven Men*, "On the road, hotels and restaurants refused service to Jackie, forcing him to eat and sleep away from the team. Letters arrived, containing death threats. Players on other teams kicked Jackie, stepped on his feet, struck him on the head with pitches, and even slashed painfully at his leg with their spikes, one time creating a seven-inch gash in his leg. Despite all of it, Jackie kept his cool."

At 28-years-old, Jackie Robinson got signed to the Brooklyn Dodgers.

The truth about a pioneer is that they can come from all different walks of life and backgrounds. As we will see, a pioneer does not only have some exterior quality that makes them great. They have a strong internal strength.

Pioneer

Overview

Life is 10% what happens to me, and 90% how I react to it.

CHUCK SWINDOLL, PASTOR, AUTHOR, AND RADIO PREACHER

The rent payment will be coming up soon, he thought to himself, as he was sorting through his family finances. Brian and his wife have two young boys and live in Southern California. Brian is 23-years-old. In early 2016, as he was reading PBY, he got a tug on his heart to pioneer.

Brian is a mix of everything digital. He knows how to code websites, design, and brand companies, his personal favorite. He had a very distant dream in his mind about one day becoming a creative director. But that was on the backburner. He had to ensure the $1,400 rent payment was covered first. Plus, at the time, the goal seemed so distant, it didn't feel like a real life opportunity.

A few weeks later, things were changing at his work, and the creative director was leaving the organization. This was his chance. His heart realized this is possible. However, the organization was looking to hire from outside.

This should have upset Brian. He could have become bitter at his employer. He could have complained and morphed to his circumstances. He could have given up on himself. But, just days before, he happened to see a position posted online for a creative director role. The only challenge was that the role was in Tennessee.

For this position to happen, he would have to move his family to Tennessee. The downside to fail was huge. For him to even apply, put his family's well-being on the line. It put his relationships on the line. Most importantly, it put his belief in his calling on the line.

In that same moment, when he realized that he could no longer grow in his current organization, something sparked in his heart.

That next week Brian gave me a call and told me his action plan. Brian, in the face of fear, doubt, risk, lack, bet on his future. He applied to become creative director of the company in Tennessee. He decided to pioneer.

The History of the Term Pioneer

The history of the word pioneer is unexpectedly more relatable that I initially assumed.

The origin of the word began in the early sixteenth century. The term pioneer came into use from a Latin base, Pedo, that means pawn. How did we go from pawn to the modern definition of a pioneer as a maverick or explorer?

Let's look at its journey through time:

Pedo (Latin): A pawn; most numerous, least valuable, pedestrian or a servant (footman)

Peão (Portuguese): Footman

Pion (French): Foot Solider

(At this next point, the word became a verb)

Peon (Spanish): Working off obligation, debt

(At this next point, we start to see the modern definition begin to form)

Peonier (French): Particular foot soldier (who would march ahead of the infantry)

Pionnier (French): Develop new, create a way for others, a servant

Today, pioneer refers to one of the first to enter or settle in a new region. The word creates pictures of being the first in a place, industry, or an enterprise.

PBY's working definition for pioneer comes in a simple phrase:

What you do with what you got

In that, to be a pioneer is not to do something as much as it is to be someone. Pioneers set out to discover their purpose, have character, and search for the best version of themselves every day. A pioneer is recognized (by herself and others) by who they are (the virtues they carry), not what they have accomplished.

Pioneering Is Not

In Great by Choice, Jim Collins and his team uncover the truths surrounding questions like what role does luck play in success and how do people thrive in uncertainty. At the beginning of the book, Collins and his team outline a central point of the book. "They," Jim Collins writes about successful individuals, "had divergent outcomes principally because they displayed very different behaviors."

Jim Collins identifies behaviors that are attributed to success. He studies them and reveals that the key behaviors we attribute to success are not the sole reasons people become successful. I think the list applies the same for pioneers*.

- Pioneering is not about being the most creative
- nor is it about being a solo, one-man army
- or being the electric visionary
- or being the charming charismatic
- or being the riskiest
- or being the quickest, unguided decision-maker
- or being the most innovative

---

* This list has been paraphrased for the sake of our conversation. It still shows the same truths Collins and his team unlock in Great by Choice.

- or being on top of the next big thing or being the Batman character in a catastrophe size difficulty
- or being the smartest in the room.

To pioneer is not about being the biggest or the best in any one-character trait or absolute situation. It is much more, as our entire life is, about who we are.

Do you live to be you—when the world wants you to act a certain way, fit in a certain way, and conform to the social norms? A pioneer is one who can be themselves alongside the pressures of life to conform. Despite failures or setbacks, pioneers can withstand the pressure because of who they are not what they have done.

Preparation

As a doctor goes into an operation, there are many factors worth considering, complications that can arise, situations that can move quickly and turn for the worse. The doctor, before he walks into the operating room is prepared for all of these things. He hopes for the best and plans for the worst. All the possible equipment, tools, and procedural understandings are in the room as surgery commences. The doctor walks into an operating room with years of preparation and experience. He has prepared with intensity for all the conditions that could possibly turn against him. In the same way, the deciding factor for pioneers is the ability to take a lifetime of decisions and own them. Many people lack the ability to pioneer because they don't prepare.

Preparation is power.

Preparation is having savings before you have a reason to. It is paying off debt, so you are financially free to make decisions when they come. It is learning about parenting before you are a parent.

Your life is made of millions of decisions. You get the option to be intentional about your day, week, month, and year. Pioneers make very deliberate decisions in seemingly irrelevant times.

Substance

A pioneer confronts danger, turbulent times, and uncharted territory with predetermined principles (character) that have already been established.

Pioneers show up, fail, get back up, and try again. Resilience isn't something you are born with. It is something you build, and it must be interwoven into the core of a pioneer.

People will laugh at pioneers. They will criticize pioneers. They will undermine pioneers. Friends and family will question pioneers. It's part of being a pioneer.

Word: Ousia (Greek: οὐσία)
Pronounciation: oo-see'-ah
Greek Definition:
Substance; essence; estate
Etymology: ous (to be) + ia (is)
Ousia, the basic element of something,
refers to its value.

The very basic element of anything. When, in the Prodigal Son story, the boy asks for his inheritance, he asks for his Ousia.
In the story, he spends it frivolously in the streets and in the night. When he comes to himself, he realizes his substance (quality living) was much more than money but in who he was. His Ousia was in an inheritance of wealth until he realized that is estate was bigger than that. It had him running back to the father.

Resilience means that despite every negative thought, action, failure, and weakness, you get back up.

Overall, the pioneer—the spirit they possess—is one of substance.

Do You Have Experience?

When a new job seeker goes for an interview, she is asked about her experience. Experience will prove that she is qualified for the role.

Pioneers take what they have been given and produce a high-return. Thus, most pioneers venture into new 'jobs' with little to no experience, at all!

If Eliab asked little David, what experience do you have fighting Goliath—a giant human with abnormal strength, David would have never had been qualified. Yes, he had faced wild animals, but that didn't qualify him to kill a man the likes of Goliath with a slingshot.

Pioneers don't need the reassurance of experience at an HR department. You cannot create a genuine future if you do not do something new. You do not need anyone's approval or validation to be a pioneer.

Outbeat Your Current Best

What makes this so real is when you understand that pioneering is not about all these things you don't have, you stop making excuses, and you make a commitment to yourself that it is possible. If your focus goes from what you cannot control, to what you can control (that is, your becoming the best version of yourself), your top priority is to outbeat your current best.

Things in your control: Your character, your decisions, your ability to create, your future, your time, your dedication, your words, your resources, and your journey.

Internal freedom is the best gauge of path and direction. You can become free internally while working a very constricting job or you can be internally free while you quit your only paying job. In either case, your freedom is of the highest importance.

This helps you stay in your lane and achieve massive success in unexpected ways as you pioneer your lane.

What a Pioneer Is

Let's look at those ten items again through a new lens.
Pioneering:

- is not being the most creative.
  It's about creating in your every day.
- is not being a solo, one-man army.
  It's about being in community.
- is not being the electric visionary.
  It's about understanding your calling with conviction.
- is not being the charming charismatic.
  It's about knowing your value.
- is not being the riskiest. It's about being vigilant at all times, especially with quick decisions.
- is not being a quick, unguided decision-maker.
  It's about being ridiculously prepared.
- is not being the most innovative.
  It's about persistence (99U's Scott Belsky wrote a whole book on it called Making Ideas Happen)
- is not being on top of the next big thing.
  It's about the small, seemingly insignificant consistencies, every day.
- is not being the Batman character in the dark night heroic. It's about doing your best.
- And it is not about being the smartest, either.
  It's about you being YOU!

Culture Asks

It is not the movement of the clock that produces the newness of life. It is the movement in your mind.

T. D. JAKES, A WORLD-RENOWNED PASTOR WHO BEGAN HIS MINISTRY AT THE AGE OF TWENTY-THREE

Success has always been hard to define.

Maybe it's a lot of money or a respectable position or the things you own. Many chase an image of 'success' or winning that is undefined.

It's hard to pinpoint how we will know when we reach success. Many people define success in different ways.

To be a pioneer, life asks us to identify what success looks like for us. There are potholes to look out for. They are, it's easy, to complain, to adopt the wrong narrative, and to morph to unexpected circumstances. On the other hand, it's hard to build skyscrapers. The gift of a pioneer is to identify what is easy to do and stop countering his progress while intentionally doing what is hard that is keeping him from his goals.

The Path of Least Resistance

When you confront something new, bigger than what you have done before, a place of improvement, a change from your current habit, or anything that in general will call you to grow, your brain signals turn to ask the exact same question, every time. That is, "How do I do this with the least amount of effort?"

This is our brain trying to protect us. It is trying to 'help' by saving us from grief, pain, and heartache. Nothing in life can be achieved on the path of least resistance.

We are called to create our future and this calls us to pioneer. And, at times, pioneers must push beyond the path of least resistance.

There may be pain, agony, heartache and uncertainty along the whole journey. Most of it will be mental tension. The knee jerk reaction of least resistance is not the best route. It isn't useful. It seems easy, but it is costly.

Do you wonder why so many people seem passionless and ineffective lives? It comes down to how people deal with change.

In a world where we are set to live longer, where we will spend more of our hours in leisure, and where food is anywhere and everywhere, we must be able to fight for what we desire. Pioneers know one thing that helps them push past this:

Anything good we aspire to bring forth is not unintentionally our desire. The desires are placed within us. Therefore, we can achieve them.

Life will test our desire. If you truly want something for good reason, the challenges you face to achieve it will reveal if you are willing to go the extra mile for them. That is, if you will bring forth the quality necessary to accomplish your desire.

The path of most resistance is probably a better choice.

Complaining

In that, it becomes very easy to complain. Because, when challenges and hardship and difficulty come, people will be persuaded to complain about their situation because it doesn't seem to fit.

Have you ever been with someone who always has a problem? Inevitably, as every problem gets solved, they locate a new problem to latch on to.

In 2015 I was working a fun marketing job. We had recently hired a new director, and I become one of her direct reports. For the story sake, let's call the new hire Brittany. During her second week on the job, our director was out of town.

Brittany, for the next two weeks, made my life a living hell. She was unsettled in the way things operated. I would sit in her office for less than twenty minutes and walk out with fifteen new tasks.

It was if, against my will, I kept going back up to the buffet line at an all-you-can-eat restaurant. My plate was overfilled and twenty minutes could compound into holding two or three plates full of food. I never had time to finish it. This problem was taking all of my focus to handle. I would go home and think about what I could do, I called friends, and I even had to have extra prayer sessions during work to get through the day. This lady, who came out of nowhere, had given my life a new set of challenges.

For reasons I will never understand, on Brittany's third week, she made a decision to leave the company. My biggest problem had just kindly exited the building. Within just days, I had been put under fire and then suddenly, my problem was gone.

When I heard the news, I sat back at my best, with a very neutral feeling. I wasn't happy. I wasn't sad.

My biggest problem was gone. What a relief.

Moments later, I found myself mentally searching for the next biggest problem to focus on. My next biggest stressor coming in at second place showed up right away. In that instant, my life changed because I realized what I had just done.

I pulled out my notebook and started writing out the scenario.

Do you realize that I pinned myself to any nearby problem to find room to complain about life?! I had just had my only concern for the last three weeks disappear, and my mind was already wandering off onto the next problem to latch onto. It's always easier to complain than it is to do the work, find the good in your situation, or utilize your resources for a high return.

We have the option to complain about what is. We also have the option to latch onto what is good.

The Narrative You Adopt

Your boss is unfair. You begin to see everything your boss does—despite their kindness, through the lens of biased, prejudiced, and wrong.

Life is too expensive. You begin to see everything as overpriced—even when you get a good deal and can afford a good life, through the lens of expensive, for the rich, and not for me.

The story you engage with is either a productive or a harmful strategy. This is self-sabotage. When you willfully sabotage what is in front of you to adapt a narrative that suites apathy and complacency.

The heart of a pioneer is to respond out of gratitude. Telling ourselves bad narratives will jeopardize our ability to step beyond our current struggle and pioneer.

Skyscrapers

Some of the world's tallest buildings reveal beautiful landscapes. You can be in New York, Dubai, or Singapore, and skyscrapers offer beautiful views of the city. Yet, they all are built with the same foundational nature.

Skyscrapers are built with certain parameters, reinforcements, and most importantly, a solid foundation. Because of the risk of the smallest failure in a skyscraper, engineers must eliminate as many potential failures as possible. They need to handle the weight of the second floor as much as the weight of the seventy-fifth floor. They must be able to sway with the wind accordingly so they aren't put under too much stress.

Further, each skyscraper is built according to the adjustments of its environment. In Tokyo, skyscrapers are susceptible to high decibel earthquakes. In Dubai, the Burj Khalifa, the world's tallest building, is specially designed to handle heavy winds. This becomes especially important as altitude increases. The entire building will suffer high levels of stress if it is not built to withstand the pressures of its environment.

Sound familiar?

To build a skyscraper, like you build your life, you need to build something that has the capacity to withstand all of the environments pressure. That means if you are in Seoul or Los Angeles, Singapore or Dubai, pioneers must be able to resist the forces of nature.

Chase the Fears

Each and every one of you must make sacrifices to become a hero possessed of courage and intrepidity. Then only shall we all be able to enjoy the freedom.

AUNG SAN, BURMA'S REVOLUTIONIST, ASSASSINATED IN 1967 FOR BELIEVING IN FREEDOM

When the disciples had pleaded with Jesus, "Teacher, do you not *care*...?" fear took over. It was their time to demonstrate courage and strength. For the first time, they were entrusted to believe in themselves. This had pushed them to their limits.

How do we escape the power of fear from keeping us from our purpose?

Our ability to transform ourselves in the hopes that we will be able to use our transformation to positively impact others is one of the most important elements of life. The way we can get to any goal in our purpose is by chasing the fears.

Ordinary Courage

Today, modern courage takes form in an office, a coffee shop, or on a street corner.

"While many of our favorite paradigms and exemplars of courage are cases of almost unbelievable endurance or bravery in the face of danger, the virtue is as much at home in the cottage as in the castle, in the office as on the battlefield... courage can be manifested in quite ordinary circumstances," wrote Geoffrey Scarre in his book, On Courage.

Word: Courage (Greek: θαρσέω)
Pronounced: kur-ij
Greek Definition: The quality of a person to face hardship, pain, and risk; to take heart
Etymology: cor (heart) + age (the outcome of; the remains of)

In a very literal sense, courage means the outcome of the heart. Courage reflects what remains of the heart when hardship, pain, and risk surround your life. Courage reveals that what was to separate us from God and harm us, is incapable. To use what is remaining, often in our lowest points, is where we develop our quality as individuals.

Courage comes in the form of physical bravery as much as mental, moral, and social, emotional, and spiritual. Courage comes at times in the most difficult circumstances. Courage in our journey allow us the opportunity to chase our fears. This is the only way you can persevere for your purpose.

The road to modern courage, despite all our contemporary advancements like health care and technology, rest where we are called to chase our fears. Modern courage is moral courage. We are responsible for transforming our life. In today's world, emotional intelligence is in demand more than the courage required for the battlefield. Our front lines that we have to face are feelings of doubt, insecurity, and weakness. We must do this to overcome depression and anxiety and to face our deepest fears.

Ordinary courage means chasing the fears in your home, office, classroom, and in your personal journey to catch your desires.

Pioneers and Fear

A pioneer does not disband fear. Rather, a pioneer steps into fear. A pioneer knows that fear is almost never escapable. Fear, in good measure, is a clear indicator that one is heading in the direction they ought.

Do pioneers have fear? All the time.

The difference between a pioneer and one who settles is that a pioneer resolves to face their fear.

To Chase the Fears

If you know the enemy and know yourself you need not fear the results of a hundred battles.

SUN TZU

The defining moment is not what happens to you, but what happens inside of you. When you can transform yourself—in hopes to bring a positive impact to others – you will set out to do your best work.

In Part II of the book, we wrote down our top fears. It's now time to bring out that list and learn how to chase the fears:

1. Understand the fear: Make sure you identify the root of the fear. Do this by asking what are you afraid of. Then ask 'why?' And, then ask, where did this fear come from? What makes this fear so real? Are you afraid of losing your reputation? Are you afraid of being judged? Are you afraid you will fail? This may take time and a moment of introspection, but it will be worth it. This will help you identify what triggers your fear.

2. Take One Step: Too often, we put more pressure on ourselves to perform at a standard that is 10x our current level or ability.

   For instance, imagine you have a fear of public speaking. You understand that the fear is because you are afraid of making a mistake. Ask yourself: what if I did make one mistake, while I am on stage, will it be fatal? Most likely not. Then ask, what if I made a ton of mistakes, would that be fatal? Again, probably not. In this way, you are taking away the power of the fear. Inasmuch, start with speaking to fifty people, not 10,000. Then, graduate to the next level of challenge. Speak to one hundred people, 500 people or 1,000 people. Often we see people who can speak to 10,000 with poise and vigor and want to be able to do that right away. This is a gradual confrontation process. The key is to never let fear dominate.

Realistically, any time you begin something new, you will look funny the first time around. Just as a baby starts to walk, she falls a few times. Get up, do it again. It's often cuter than you think.

Hint: Look for pieces of your character that are being called to grow through the fear. There will always be a connection to your character and fear. The fear of being judged, for example, is usually tied to our inner quality of humility (understanding our place with God). That is, a person is afraid of being judged because the way people may respond to what they do. In light of this, our humility will call us to realize that this act (whatever it is) is to serve other people. It is bigger than just that individual.

3. There is no better state of success than measuring your progress to overcome fear. The most challenging part is finding a way to accurately measure your wins.

First, write down, to the best of your ability, the fear you have come to understand. Write it on a new piece of paper in a notebook, in an email that is self-directed, or a note on your device. In any case, you need something that you can access any time.

Second, write down exactly what next step you are going to take to chase the fear. What will you have to do to challenge the fear? It may be doing something uncomfortable. Not to fret. Keep it simple. This should be something you can do within the next day (if not today). Finally, track progress by writing two or three sentences about any success or failure. This will allow you identify what triggers the fear and help you confront it. The main goal is grabbing a better understanding of the fear, why it comes, and its true size. The more you realize what is happening in regards to fear, the more you are able to take on the battle.

I created a little motto to go into my day. This paragraph helps me realize that fear isn't so big and that chasing the fears is worth all our effort.

Our Manifesto

Be ready to fail today. Be ready to look ridiculous.
Be ready to grow. Define success by becoming your best self.
You get the chance to do your best because fear can't hold
you back. This is bigger than you and your week.
This is bigger than yesterday. Think large. You have barely
reached your potential. Experiment. Try again.
Never let up. Change. Stake your claim. Act a fool.
Take risks. Love your life. In everything, press forward toward
freedom. There is no other route. Pioneer your future.
It's more important than money.
Don't take yourself so seriously. He already did.

Chase the fears.

The wellspring of courage and endurance in the face of unbridled power is generally a firm belief in the sanctity of ethical principles (character) combined with a historical sense that despite all setbacks the condition of man is set on an ultimate course for both spiritual and material advancement.

Aung San Suu Kyi,
Politician and opposition leader of Myanmar

You will never do anything in this world without courage. It is the greatest quality of the mind next to honor.

Aristotle

Courage is a praiseworthy
quality in itself,
but it is at its best only
where it is summoned
to serve morally fine ends
for their own sake.

Geoffrey Scarre

Accountability

Honesty is more than not lying. It is truth telling, truth speaking, truth living, and truth loving.

JAMES FAUST, RELIGIOUS LEADER

Imagine, you went to buy juice, and the juice bottle said 100 percent juice. But it wasn't. When you went to the gas station, you were choosing between unleaded and premium. You choose premium, you paid the higher price, but instead of pumping gas, the machine pumped vegetable oil. What about when you pay for a flight to go on a trip, just to land, and end up in an entirely different country from your intended destination?

If this were how the world operated, we would all walk around like paranoid activists constantly double checking and questioning everything.

One of the most powerful tools you have as an individual is the community around you, both professionally and personally.

In the same way, every public company hires accountants to manage, track, and record the books for ultimate transparency, accountability holds keys to your success that few realize.

What makes your life any different?

Reaching Your Full Potential

There are two things you need to reach your full potential.

Firstly, God.

You need God to reach your full potential. It's like trying to win a NASCAR race and not having a vehicle to actually race. There are things He can do in the spiritual realm that must be done for you to reach your full potential. It's something even a billion dollars, a staff of 5,000, or a hundred acre property cannot buy.

Secondly, accountability.

When you have others hold you to your word, you are leveraging powerful forces to make sure you stay true. It's easier to make a commitment to God in the heat of a moment than it is to keep it.

In a moment of drive or determination, you can make an awesome life-changing decision. What ends up happening is that things get hard. Last month's excitement can easily be forgotten by this month's dealings.

When they get hard, it becomes very easy to switch courses and lose all the traction you gained. In the middle, where it is toughest, accountability will help you stay the course. Your drive isn't dependable because it's an emotion. It is much easier to make a determined decision for a lifetime of life-giving value than it is to keep that decision.

When you know that you will be accountable for all your actions today, in a particular area of your life, you will be much more likely to stay the course, than if you are free to make a new decision every day.

What is Accountability?

Glad you asked.

Well, you are, with breathing room, allowed to do whatever you want. Every day, you get to decide what you want to do. Accountability is simply accounting for your ability. Public companies account for their finances, business, and goals. Many people struggle with their finances, business, and goals. What is interesting is that making one purchase at a public company for less than a $1,000 seems so tiny in comparison to the overall operation. Yet, billion dollar companies track $1,000 purchases. Why? Because it is small purchases that uncover the true cost of doing business, keep the companys' actions in check, and determine if the business is heading in its desired direction.

You wouldn't realize that the smallest moments shape your life unless you took into account the ability these moments make to define you.

Accountability is simply holding record with someone over a specific area of your life like finances, professional goals, personal goals, or one-off situations that need improvement, like public speaking or moderate eating.

Accountability Leads to Freedom

Freedom is more of a danger if responsibility is not concurrent.

It's like electricity. When you turn a light on by flipping the switch, you allow a current of energy to bypass from the source to the bulb. In our life, our households have proper lighting because every bit of electricity that we use is governed by some type of switch.

The power in your life must also be governed by some type of switch. Your level of authority is often connected to your level of responsibility. Your freedom to live out in your life comes from transparency.

You have the opportunity to shine bright when the electricity (the power of your life) is focused and directed in a particular bulb (situation).

Accountability is the switch. It keeps you govern an attempt to dismantle the danger of being shocked.

The Harsh Reality

Be honest with yourself and others. You jeopardize every part of your accountability the moment you are not fully honest. Most people lie to themselves, again and again, and again. This only leads to self-sabotage. Culturally, sharing your bank statement with someone is unorthodox. If it helps you gain financial freedom and it keeps you in check in your spending, please, do it. Drop the cultural norms and give yourself the freedom you deserve. Rather, take the freedom you deserve by simply being honest, not cordial.

Be truthful despite failure or shame, it has a lot of power to bring to light what is hidden.

But all things become visible when they are exposed to the light, for everything that becomes visible is light.

This will confront the 'new' syndrome. It's much easier to start a new project, fantasize about your dreams, or buy domain names than it is to complete a project, chase your dreams, or create/code a website.

Types of Accountability

Anything you want to show consistency in or be responsible for, you want accountability for, especially if it poses a challenge. The best way to get rid of bad habits that you have had for five, eight, or ten years is with accountability.

Personal accountability: if you deal with stealing, jealousy, complaining, gossip, lustful thoughts and actions, cheating, procrastination, greed, lying, binge eating, wasting time, or lack of spiritual discipline in the areas of reading, worshiping, or praying.

Professional accountability: if you deal with bad habits, never reaching your goals, starting more projects than you can finish, missing deadlines, saying yes to more than you can handle, always being busy, not saving, lack of focus, always doubting yourself, living in fear, apathy, or complacency.

Start with the top priorities, your biggest challenges, or start with your smallest issue. In either case, do what is a worthy challenge for the season. The goal is to not do too many at the same time. It's hard to give enough attention to change your eating habits and watching too much TV and trying to find financial stability all in the same month.

Then, find someone who will hold you accountable for the next ninety days. Find someone you can trust that is open with you, and you can be straight with, especially when you fail. You can have a quick chat every day where you review three to four questions in less than ten minutes. Or, it can be a conversation for thirty minutes, once a week to review a three to five-point checklist. Or, it can be biweekly in a one hour meet up. In any case, do something that will challenge you and make sure you confront your habit changing course frequently enough that it doesn't get forgotten. Changing habits takes focus and focus takes energy. Make sure that you have clearly defined goals and checklists. What do you want to be held accountable toward? If it is a fear (or something that is hard to measure directly), use something you can do every day like speaking up in a meeting or sharing the gospel with someone every day as a goal to make sure you are headed in the right direction. You can start with daily goals, go to weekly, then monthly. Because, as you progress, you tend to incline yourself toward your goals more and more. Once you do it, and you no longer feel the urge to go in the wrong direction, it will become subconscious.

Don't put all these on one person. It's a lot of work. Seek out multiple people who are successful at what you want to be held accountable for and ask them. Make sure you do this at your pace. There is no reason to try and take off going 300 mph like a commercial jet when you are only flying a small aircraft. It takes much less energy to launch.

There are three rules:

Rule #1: Make no excuse

Rule #2: Always tell the truth

Rule #3: Never lose sight of rule 1 & 2

In this way, you are sure to succeed.

My final note of encouragement with accountability: do it today, and when you fail, be honest. Because when you are honest, you make it easier to just get back up and walk it out again. Failure will happen. The goal isn't perfection, but growth. Get back up, you've got this.

"For you were formerly darkness, but now you are Light in the Lord; walk as children of Light (for the fruit of the Light consists in all goodness and righteousness and truth), trying to learn what is pleasing to the Lord. Do not participate in the unfruitful deeds of darkness, but instead even expose them... But all things become visible when they are exposed by the light, for everything that becomes visible is light.

Ephesians 5 New American Standard Bible (NASB)

Challenger: Apathy and Complacency

Life is never made unbearable by circumstances, but only by lack of meaning and purpose.

VIKTOR FRANKL, SURVIVOR OF THE HOLOCAUST,
PRISONER OF WAR IN AUSCHWITZ

Sometime between the moment when I ordered dinner over the phone and when it was rolled into my living room like a corpse on a rubber-wheeled table, I lost all interest in it.

TENNESSEE WILLIAMS IN *THE CATASTROPHE OF SUCCESS*

At one point in my corporate career, I went through a season of grumbling and protest. I was completely unhappy. Even though I enjoyed the work and the people, something inside of me was off.

I was unhappy because I felt I was being undervalued. I knew I was capable of doing more good for the Kingdom, for my family, and for my future.

I tried to negotiate a better work schedule with my company as a short-term fix. I submitted a three-page proposal and went from having one day offsite to two days offsite.

The day after this happened, I was excited. But my excitement wore off quickly. I still felt undervalued. I couldn't quit because it wasn't the right time to transition 100 percent away from the company yet.

That is when I began to become apathetic and complacent. I became eager in spirit, but lazy in action. Then, I began to not care about my personal goals, like paying down school loans and starting my own side projects. I was disheartened by the fact that I knew there was more in me, but I couldn't realize it.

When no one sees your value or understands your worth, do you have the courage to bring that into existence?

Your ability to change the world begins within yourself. Do you have the courage to chart your own journey? To build the inner freedom and sovereignty that, despite devaluation or disrespect, you walk with your courage and heart lifted in an act of complete escape from your external circumstances. To determine your life from an internal stance is seldom experienced by people voluntarily.

Apathy Defined

Apathy = the suppression of passion, emotions, and excitement; a cold, disinterest in life; indifference towards what is good and hopeful in your world; a feeling of emptiness that reigns supreme over your life.

Apathy leads to high levels of complaining, self-pity, and wallowing. Apathy is not a state of struggling to make a decision as much as it is a state of disinterest in the results of any action.

Combat Apathy

To combat apathy, figure out what your ideal Monday would look like. For many, Monday marks the start of another dreadful work week.

With such clarity and detail and scheduling, picture your most precious Monday. Figure that out. Once you do, I want you to make a comparison.

Compare what your current Monday looks like to your future Monday. What do you have to change to get there? If it is a new job, learn how you will make that happen. Maybe you spend time on the weekends applying to other jobs so you can transform your Monday.

Maybe it is a lifestyle of travel and creating. How do you transform your current Monday? You can start learning about the countries you want to visit, paying off debt, and grow a travel savings account.

This way, you can turn the most dreadful day of the week into your dream.

Complacency Defined

A self-satisfying zone. Where we position our area of action to favor our area of comfort, our comfort zone. It is a self-pleasing mechanism. We make future decisions based on our past experiences.

Complacency draws us away from going above and beyond our past milestones. How can we ever outbeat our current best if we allow complacency to rule?

Complacency is what keeps us doing the same bad habits we dislike.

Combat Complacency

If you find yourself doing remedial work through the day to feel successful (checking email all day, social media, or getting all the small projects out of the way), and pushing away more meaningful projects, it's time to challenge your values.

What you do each day is a clear sign of what you value. If you say you value living your purpose, you ought to be intentional about your days and hours.

Your Darkest Season Is Your Brightest Light

We have seen how our greatest struggles are tied to our greatest freedoms. We have seen how our doubts indicate the path we ought to travel. We have seen how our greatest fears are tied to our greatest hopes. In all of this, what we must realize is that our darkest seasons are undeniably tied to our brightest lights.

When I discovered that my purpose is unconditional—I mean really discovered this truth—my life was completely going downhill.

At the time, it was my first year after graduating college. I was working a job I had no interest in and I was slowly being terminated. During the final month of my employment, I started asking myself important questions like what would I do every day, despite a paycheck? What would I do if I had a million dollars in my bank account? What would I do I started something new today?

From then on out, I have made a pact with myself to always give my dream time and devotion. Not because it is some get rich scheme or some power play. I am truly hungry and convinced that life is experienced best when we know we are living out the design we were created to bring forth.

My art is writing. My love is writing. I will write whether ten publishers pick me up or none. I will write whether people enjoy my writing or not. Because, for me, writing is a process of developing clarity in my life. It has helped me make sense of this amazing and uncontrollable world.

When everything tells you to give up, I hope you believe that maybe, just maybe, that dark, gloomy season could actually become a light for you in the future. A light in the direction you should go. A light for others to follow. A light that makes Kingdom living amazing.

How Does This Change Your Life?

One should not search for an abstract meaning of life. Everyone has his own specific vocation or mission in life to carry out a concrete assignment which demands fulfillment. Therein he cannot be replaced, nor can his life be repeated. Thus, everyone's task is as unique as is his specific opportunity to implement it.

VIKTOR FRANKL, SURVIVOR OF THE HOLOCAUST,
PRISONER OF WAR IN AUSCHWITZ

At Princeton University, two psychologists, John Darley and Daniel Batson, conducted a study they titled "From Jerusalem to Jericho." The study was based on the story of the Good Samaritan where Jesus explains that a beaten traveler is overlooked by a priest and a Levite only to be cared for by the most unsuspecting character of all, a Samaritan. The study asked if people are in a hurry, will they overlook their ability to help those around them in need, especially with this story fresh in their minds?

The students were asked to prepare a talk given a Biblical theme, the Good Samaritan. Following the Bible study, the seminar students were told to hurry up and walk to another building to give their talk.

When the students were getting ready to head to the building where they would give their talk, the psychologists informed some of the students that they were running late. Other students were told that they could take their time getting over to the next building.

A man was strategically placed on the students walk to the other building. He was positioned to be in distress. He was instructed to cough and appear down trodden.

The experiment, as it was set out, in the most opportune moment (as someone who just read the parable of the Good Samaritan), was to investigate peoples' heightened awareness of a topic from their sermon and the context of their situation. Our first prediction would be yes, students who have the story of the Good Samaritan fresh in their minds would be more inclined and salient to show compassion to the man in distress. Secondly, we would predict these individuals, as they had dedicated their lives (as students in theology) to a life of following Christ, would find this moment one of obvious consideration. Finally, the study asked what role does 'hurry' play in the decision for these seminar students and their actions of faith?

Out of the different groups of people in the study, which group decided to stop and help the person in distress?

The study came to show that individuals who felt in a hurry were highly unlikely to stop. On average, people in a hurry were only likely to help one out of ten times. Having the story of the Good Samaritan fresh in their heads did very little to change this outcome. One student literally stepping over the man in distress. These seminary students were going to a room to preach about helping those in distress as they overlooked the trouble in front of them!

Today, over thirty years after the experiment took place, we are busier than ever. An average person can now achieve more in a day than an average person could a century ago. As Malcolm Gladwell so well paraphrased this experiment, "What this study is suggesting, in other words, is that the convictions of your heart and the actual contents of your thoughts are less important, in the end, in guiding your actions than the immediate context of your behavior." In a world of ever-increasing efficiency, it's important to know our journey is of urgency, not haste. The difference is life-changing.

Thus, the power to become a pioneer is not in some far off land or large dream, but what you can do today to realize one step of proximity closer to your dream, even if you may not find your current situation so favorable.

Fundamentally YOU

Rose Han was interning at a public relations agency in Los Angeles while she was completing her marketing degree. When she graduated at twenty-two, she realized the business world wasn't what she wanted (or, that she really wanted to be an actress). She decided to pioneer. She took on her responsibilities to earn a living while giving herself the flexibility to pursue an acting career.

DeEdwin decided to join the Navy. He was twenty-two years old and wanted to take the next step in his life. Actually, he was more exhausted from not reaching his full potential. When he was halfway through the two-hour drive to the recruitment office in San Diego, he realized that the Navy wasn't what he truly wanted to do. The Navy seemed like the right choice because of the wrong reasons. Maybe to fill the human desire for significance or adding value to the world, he discovered that the Navy wasn't the right decision for him. He turned around and that same week he signed up for hairdressing academy.

Natalia has worked hard to become a young marketing guru. At twenty-four years old, she puts in work. When her corporate job wasn't satisfying her, and she could finish her job during the 40-hour work week, she made a decision to start her own agency.

The day Rose left the PR agency she pioneered. She walked into uncharted waters. The day DeEdwin signed up for hairdresser school he pioneered. He walked into an unknown future. The day Natalia left her corporate career to start her own business, she pioneered. She walked into the high chance of failure. Each of them stepped into a future that was uncertain and unpredictable.

Every decision above took an internal shift to made an external change. It was an internal acceptance of potential downside in light of one thing: these young people are discovering who they are.

Your journey must be fundamentally you. Not what your parents, teachers, or social pressure expect from you. It's not what the world calls from you, either. It is much more what life calls from you. The person-specific ideals and challenges that you must confront.

Identify theft is when someone takes your identity. It's almost like there are two of you. In God's eyes, he made only one of you. Why would you not be fundamentally you?

Our situation is so much more about doing the best with your screwed-up family, financial situation, and current working position—all while making sure you are not giving the world a fake version of you, but the real version of you.

To build your own dream requires you to break free of excuses that hinder you from your purpose.

Is it difficult? Yes. Is it scary? Yes. Will you fail? Yes. Is it worth it? YES

Rest On the Layover

If something does not go your way, how do you respond? If you are put in a position where you no longer enjoy your work or you are no longer interested in your degree, how do you respond? Do you quit immediately?

For many, the best advice is to quit. Why would you stay someplace you don't enjoy? However, the Bible gives the only logical step toward stepping in faith and trusting God to work through a situation. For a believer, it's not smart to leave the airport when you are waiting for a connecting flight. You wait—even if it feels like forever.

Likewise, it is unwise to wait when you have yet to buy a connecting flights ticket.

Above all, keep your relationship with God priority and follow through with the legwork necessary to pioneer your future.

Your journey with God gives you priority booking (grace on your travel). Don't forget that. If you are on the layover or buying a ticket to a new location, remember to rest on the layover.

The Epiphany

When we feel like giving up, we feel like a brand new person.

It all comes to a changed mindset. The challenge is that organic. It happens when it happens. It cannot be mustered up. It is something you must decide on.

Many people may not believe in you. That is fine. It may even be those closest to you that run you away from your dreams. They tell you it's risky. They tell you might fail. They tell you that you should think about it again. But when God gives you a dream, what you have to do, despite every type of setback, is believe in your calling.

Believe in your dreams. Believe in your desires. Believe in your ability to overcome. Believe in the future. Believe in your company. Believe in people.

This is much harder to do at a younger age (but oh so worth it). It's difficult because you usually feel that you have little to offer and little on which to base your stamina. But how else will you build the stamina?

Free To Chase

You are outbeating your current best. Again and again. You can get more with less. You build consistent intentionality. Your acuity and insight will magnify in the most insignificant situations. You are free to chase purpose despite all of life's constrictions and challenges. Provided that, what can you accomplish today, this year, and in ten years by beginning your pioneer journey now?

We are afflicted in every way, but not crushed; perplexed, but not driven to despair; persecuted, but not forsaken; struck down, but not destroyed; always carrying in the body the death of Jesus, so that the life of Jesus may also be manifested in our bodies.

Second Epistle to the Corinthians

Go! Guide

This section below is an in-depth analysis of characteristics around discipline that allow you to thrive in any discipline practice. There is additional material at purposebuiltyoung.com/resources.

The idea that we can just snap our fingers and replace them with a new one [routine] is naive. Learning essential new skills is never easy. But once we master them and make them automatic we have won an enormous victory, because the skill remains with us for the rest of our lives. The same is true with routines. Once they are in place they are gifts that keep on giving.

ESSENTIALISM, BY GREG MCKEOWN

Keep a Diary

Men, you can call it a track log. In either case, do it. See your progress. Just because it's personal doesn't mean that you have to keep it that way. Track it. Have your accountability have access to it. Use a google excel sheet. Mark a big X every time you succeed at your goal. You will start to see a lot more success than failure.

One note here: don't beat yourself up if you fall off one day. Discipline is a marathon, not a sprint. More people fail because they beat themselves up more than being incapable of achieving the goal. If you fail—you binge eat, watch TV, or drink a cup of coffee—the best thing you can do is get back up and forget it. You have too much to gain to focus on one tiny loss. Binge eating usually takes less than two hours. We often give up our dreams for a two-hour mistake versus internalizing the progress we have made over the last month.

Keep Track

Keep track of common threads in your life, as well as notice how your thinking is changing. We must change our thinking often. We must challenge our thinking. Getting it on paper allows us to actually revisit our thinking in a new sphere outside of minds.

I make it a point to journal every day, first thing in the morning. I could write one sentence or three pages. It doesn't matter. I just have to write something. Even if you are not a writer, this will help you clarify you thoughts and what God is doing in your life and what doubts fill your mind. This will help you reflect. This will help inspire you to grow. This will help you see subconscious threads in your thinking. After reviewing a three-month period of notes, I discovered that I was such a hard critic on myself.

The Art of the Twenty-One-Day Challenge

Refrain (fast) from _____ today. (Options could be: one meal, one snack, one TV show, one coffee, caffeine in general, one daily comfort). You should make it a practice to refrain from something every day. In a world of so much, it is easy to be overindulgent and not even notice it. How does teach you to be in control of yourself?

Use this challenge to encourage yourself to fast from one thing for twenty-one days. While you are doing it, examine yourself and identify what triggers come up that make you crave the thing you gave up. If you are struggling, it is good advice to take five minutes (which will feel like a lifetime) to sit quietly, not doing anything else, and embrace the urge. Identify what is causing you to really want to have a cup of coffee, a check on social media, or a piece of desert. You might find out the urge is easier to resist than you thought.

Often, the things that trigger us to self-sabotage are unconscious, emotional triggers. We are tired, fatigued, or angry. You can use the process of self-discovery above to identify the queues and use those triggers to do something else. Instead of reaching for a bag of chips to binge on, you reach for a bag of carrots to satisfy that crunch you want.

Do a twenty-one-day challenge once a month. Imagine where you will be in a six months. Image where you will be in just twelve months? Imagine how different your life will be in twenty-four months?

Create Deadlines

The hardest part of our faith is when we are stuck between two decisions. What does success look like, without self at the center? Should I go to college (because my parents want me to) when I want to be a photographer? Do I quit this job (with no income to replace it)? Do I date this guy (when he is not fully on board with Jesus)? We often assume these answers are easy. They are not. No real questions of life come easy. They shouldn't.

Set deadlines. A deadline is a moment in time that has three features:

· Feature 1: A deadline gives you space to think a lot before making a final decision. (In that, it actually counters our natural tendency to make a decision and then change it again and again). It allows all the emotions of a bad day or panic to disseminate. When the smoke settles, do you still wait to step forward or back?

- Feature 2: A deadline will be a final decision. If you say yes, then it is yes. You do not switch the decision again. You stand strong in that decision. The same thing happens if it is a no. You make a decision to act. A decision to move forward on something, and why you made that decision.

- Feature 3: A deadline allows you to freely fail. If you make a mistake, you don't regret it. You make a decision to act. And from that day forward, you move confidently in that step.

In summary, the confidence that a deadline gives you is worth it.

I remember when I was struggling with a new manager at my job. At the time, I was working in a temporary position and trying to get hired. She was giving me a mighty hard time during her first week on the job. I tried to stay up with the work, but it was high remedial and task-driven. Plus, it questioned my position at the company where I had a fairly good standing with the other executives. I wanted to quit and try my own thing. Be an entrepreneur. Make my own money.

Eventually, I set a deadline. I told myself, in a month, I will make a decision to either stay with the company or leave the company. The day I needed to make the decision, I was offered the job.

The beauty of a deadline is that it gives you room to think freely. If God does not care about you failing or you succeeding, then he cares about your heart. Your heart is a place where heaven and earth meet. Letting God take on this approach in your life will make all the difference.

For the disciplinarians—Those who naturally wake up, get places on time, and find it easy to focus, make sure that every activity you do brings you closer to what you really want in life.

As you become more disciplined, the trade-offs become, as with anything, more about an internal system than an external one. As you will say yes to fewer and fewer projects, you will be overcoming internal challenges and behaviors like gossip, over-indulging, and ego. You will find yourself doing what you love throughout the day—as you are—dare I say it—living your dreams.

The thief comes with
the sole intention
of stealing and killing
and destroying,
but I came to bring
them life, and far more
life than before.

John 10:10 PHILLIPS

Human beings want to be free and however long they may agree to stay locked up, to stay oppressed, there will come a time when they say 'That's it.' Suddenly they find themselves doing something that they never would have thought they would be doing, simply because of the human instinct that makes them turn their face towards freedom.

Aung San Suu Kyi,
Politician and opposition leader of Myanmar

Conclusion

Instant Freedom

The only thing you should demand in haste is instant freedom.

Under the most undesirable circumstances, you can still claim your freedom. What this takes is a strong internal quality. In the face of catastrophe, disaster, distress, and alarm, an optimist sits with poise, calmness, and vigor, and grants himself the ability to gain freedom to:

1. Add value: Add value to those around you, to love and serve them, radically and with all your entirety. To extend generosity, expecting nothing in return. In all, to increase the level of your impact, per person, on a level of depth and engagement. It's better to impact one person on a deep level than 1,000 people on a superficial level.

2. Stop proving yourself to others: You are made with the utmost necessities and are capable of all you require. How dare someone question that. How dare someone use your level of accomplishments to measure your worth when you have your own unique, specific calling.

3. Stop pleasing others: Stop trying to gain respect from those who cannot even love themselves. We easily mix-up our obligation of loving others with an attempt of gaining respect from them. Don't waste your time, energy, or thought power to try and change others or their opinion of you. Just love them, constantly.

4. Have no restraint by constriction: We tend to see challenges as negative and weakness as unfavorable. Accomplishments tend to get in the way of what we need to do. In either case, when you can identify your struggle, you open yourself to growth. You can take on any challenge.

The world is constantly changing. If we come to grips with our own broken reality, we may find that freedom is not extended to a later date. It isn't going to come with more money. It isn't going to start from the outside, but within us in a mindset that battles for purpose and calling every day.

Conclusion

Can You Do It All Again?

Hsieh: The ultimate definition of success is you can lose everything you have and truly be ok with it.
Interviewer: Could you lose everything and be happy?
Hsieh: I think that would actually be a fun challenge.

TONY HSIEH, THE ORIGINAL CEO OF ZAPPOS, SOLD TO AMAZON IN 2009 FOR $1.2 BILLION

Janine Shepherd, a member of the Australian ski team in the upcoming Winter Olympics of 1986, had an unexpected life-threatening injury during training. Following the injury, her doctors announced she was a partial paraplegic, which eliminated her ability to participate in the Winter Olympics in Calgary, Canada in 1988. The accident took away her ability to ski, and confronted her, as life does, with a six-word question:

Can you do it all again? (CYDIAA)

Everything she was good at, everything she had been spending years training for, was ripped away from her. She was no longer able to be a part of what she had identified with. What's more, she was required to continue living with ailments that she had never expected.

In a TED talk she gave in 2012, she shared her answer to CYDIAA. "Sitting at home in my wheelchair," Janine told the crowd in Kansas City, "and my plaster body cast, an airplane flew overhead, and I looked up, and I thought to myself, 'That's it! If I can't walk, then I might as well fly.'"

Life presented her with a new task, a new calling, a new story. She didn't let the accident stop her. She got back up.

Fairy tales end with happy endings. Success stories tell of a challenge overcome. In the swing of things, life has its own way to go up and down. From the beauty we find in art to the wonderful design of a building, everything we aspire to seems to have a fairy tale ending with smiles, love, and joy.

What goes well beyond an individual's talents and character is how they deal with CYDIAA. It tells the truth of why you do what you do.

Elon Musk, after creating Paypal with another startup banking system called Confinity, was ousted from being the CEO. He was ousted while on honeymoon with his new wife. At the time, he was twenty-nine years old.

Even with the initial success of his career with Paypal, he was approached by CYDIAA.

As, he too, was figuring things out, everything he was pursuing was calling him to adapt.

He invested all his earnings and experience into what we now know as SpaceX and Tesla.

Two years later, he started SpaceX, and then two years later met two people who pitched the idea of an electric car to him. Then, the electric car called Telsa was born. In the US, the sale of large luxury vehicles was outperformed by Tesla beating Mercedes, Audi, BMW in 2015.

Telsa now has a $31 billion market cap.

Steve Jobs had met CYDIAA after he was ousted from Apple and started NeXt and Pixar. Einstein met CYDIAA often after he was continually told by his teachers he would never succeed and failed his college entrance exams. The Israelites met CYDIAA through every single hardship on their trek to the promise land.

Today, in the middle, can you lose your spot, in your education, your work, your progress, and start over? Can you lose it all, and be happy? Could you hear the world ask you to change paths completely? Can you lose the progress you made in your work, craft, or position today, and still be happy? The bottom line is, what you become in the process is more important than the dream.

The value of a good attitude is just that, it's goodness. Never let your ego get in the way of starting. Things come to sudden ends. Things change quickly. What is true is that our character is completely mobile. We can take it anywhere we go.

CYDIAA is bound to happen. What makes CYDIAA so interesting is its ability to bring out the best in us and help us realize new potential. In a world of fleeting success and arbitrary goals and temporary achievements, what do our dreams really aspire to bring forth? Is it attention? Is it admiration? Is it position? What if everything you do today was forced to change? Would you still do your best?

The question is profoundly impossible to overlook when we realize the soul question that God asks us: will you give it all up for me?

Everything means everything. Our ability to build God's Kingdom and allow him to take it away is all part of the fun of being a child of God.

As a child buys Legos to enjoy the building, not the final product, our work could get destroyed and we can start building again.

Many people live the opposite way. Like Lego building, people buy Ikea furniture only for the final product and never enjoy the building. When the building is not going as planned, they are left upset.

When things in life get destroyed, we must be able to keep our internal qualities intact. Our calling, identity, and passion aren't like Legos or Ikea furniture that are built and destroyed in a day. Our character is built in God! No matter what the external status of our life, we have an internal strength to get us through.

The true test will be if you meet CYDIAA and still be happy.

If so, I think you won.

Conclusion

The treasure which the hero fetches
from the dark cavern is life: it is himself.

C. G. JUNG, *SYMBOLS OF TRANSFORMATION*

Person-Specific

Over and over again, I have referred to this idea of person-specific calling. What this values is that no two people are the same, that everyone was created with the same worth, and that your calling must be pursued from within.

If all our time were to journey together, at the end of the day, I would not want you to only succumb to my definition and formation of purpose built young. Much more, I would habitually and repeatedly remind you to think on your own.

To do what you do because you have examined its conditions for yourself. Following a herd or a trend is blind following. It is revering the superficial accolades and hype over who you are meant to be. It's okay to be weird. It's okay to stand out. It's okay to live your dreams. And it definitely is okay for you to live to be wholly and fully you.

I love the way Alain De Botton said it at the end of his TED talk:

"So what I want to argue for is not that we should give up on our ideas of success, but we should make sure that they are our own. We should focus in on our ideas, and make sure that we own them; that we are truly the authors of our own ambitions. Because it's bad enough not getting what you want, but it's even worse to have an idea of what it is you want and find out, at the end of the journey, that it isn't, in fact, what you wanted all along."

Action Necessary

When I was a student in my second year of college, I took a music theory course. The course challenged me beyond my wildest expectations. I had no idea what a scale was, how to identify notes by ear, or the ability to understand intervals. Then, very quickly, I learned, if I do not invest lots of time into this course, I will never step up.

I spent every day doing ear training, learning about intervals (M6, m6, P5, P4... and so on). I loved it. I had just started playing piano the year before. It was making me so happy. I was getting better and better.

Then, in my second semester of music theory courses, by which time most students had dropped out, our teacher made one-point clear.

"The notes on the page are simply notes on the page. If you cannot hear them, sing them, or understand them, you are looking at black ink on the paper," she told us.

At first, it didn't click. Then, after she said it a few times, I realized what she was saying.

She was telling us that being able to read music is nice. But, we must be able to actualize it.

In other words, we must be able to know what action, dynamic, and power the sheet of music possesses. To build character means that you are able to not only understand it or experience it, but have an internal wisdom towards the precepts and disciplines of God. A life of action.

You cannot make it all the way through this book to settle for a life of inaction. You may not know the full details yet, or the power of each discipline, but it's worth chasing. Action is the only way you will find out for yourself.

Obligation

You have too much on the line to gain.
You have too much to learn.
Too much to experience.
Too much to unlock.
Too much to see.
Too much to become...
To settle.

The world needs people who act towards a cause greater than themselves. Social issues are everywhere; your help can permeate everywhere. Today, your chance to add impact to the lives around you is greater than ever before. The relevance of PBY today is that this leaves you more responsible than ever before.

Enjoy the Journey

Take off that incredibly heavy burden that makes you feel uneven, lacking, and never enough. Give up your rights that demand respect and position. There is nothing more satisfying than reaching your goal. Oh, except one thing. The journey towards that goal.

Don't make it a grueling battle. Enjoy it.

Imagine That...

If everything that exists has a cause—from a tiny insect to a single tree in the Amazon—then you have purpose. If even one thing in the world has a cause—say for instance the gravitational pull of the sun on the earth or the power of one cell to heal the body—then everything has a cause. I will say that again: EVERYTHING has a cause.

In the same way,
colored pencils are used to draw,
applications are created to engineer,
satellites are made to orbit,
pens are made to write,
coffee is made to drink,
airplanes are made to fly,
cars are made to drive,
books are made to be read,

your life is made to have Purpose Built Young.

Sharing

If this book helped you,
I encourage you, share it with a friend.

Appendix A

Biblical Foundation

Therefore, believers, be all the more diligent to make certain about His calling and choosing you [be sure that your behavior reflects and confirms your relationship with God]; for by doing these things [actively developing these virtues], YOU WILL NEVER STUMBLE [in your spiritual growth and will live a life that leads others away from sin]

2 PETER 1:10 AMP

The foundation of this book is based on key Biblical truths.

Here is a handful of promises worth laying your life toward. If you have any wrong or inaccurate thinking about one, circle it. If you know, you need to increase one, square it. Make annotations toward your current position on each. Some will be easy for you to believe, and for others, you may be more resistant. Be truthful because if this is the truth, it's worth finding out now. Here are the main ideas the book stands on.

Saving Faith

The Bible talks about salvation, that is, saving faith, is by grace through faith. PBY refers to faith regarding your faith for life's daily obligations, what we call Grind Faith. Our references through PBY to faith do not question saving faith. This helps keep everything in proper order. Here, the Bible makes it clear that salvation is not by anything we do:

> For by grace you have been saved through faith. And this is not your own doing; it is the gift of God, not a result of works, so that no one may boast.
> EPHESIANS 2:8–9

In James, we see more clarity on what our grind faith means. In the verse, the book is referring to Abraham's faith.

> You see that faith was active along with his works, and faith was completed by his works.
> JAMES 2:22

Purpose

You are born with purpose. It is so literal, concrete, and unconditional that it would make even the most seemingly unnecessary parts of life have meaning. Purpose is so real that the dust in your house was designed! Let's take a look at a few of the verses that speak this truth:

> "The purposes of a person's heart are deep waters, but one who has insight draws them out."
> PROVERBS 20:5 NIV

> The Lord will fulfill his purpose for me; your steadfast love, O Lord, endures forever. Do not forsake the work of your hands."
> PSALMS 138:8

God said to Jeremiah, the words below:

> Before I formed you in the womb I knew you, and before you were born I consecrated you; I appointed you a prophet to the nations.
> JEREMIAH 1:5

To add icing to the cake, He even said He saw everything and called it good:

> Then God said, "Let us make man in our image, after our likeness..."
> So God created man in his own image, in the image of God he created him; male and female he created them.
> And God blessed them...
> And God saw everything that he had made, and behold, it was very good.
> EXCERPTS FROM GENESIS 1:26–31

That means you have identity, calling, and are created for good works. Here is one example that confirms your calling:

> Set your heart not on riches, but on goodness, Christ-likeness, faith, love, patience, and humility. Fight the worthwhile battle of the faith, keep your grip on that life eternal to which you have been called...
> 1 Timothy 6:11b-12a PHILLIPS)

Importance of Character

Nearly every promise in the Bible is tied to character. Here is one King David recited to Solomon when he was giving him his calling:

> Now, my son, the Lord be with you, so that you may succeed in building the house of the Lord your God, as he has spoken concerning you. Only, may the Lord grant you discretion and understanding, that when he gives you charge over Israel you may keep the law of the Lord your God. Then you will prosper if you are careful to observe the statutes and the rules that the Lord commanded Moses for Israel. Be strong and courageous. Fear not; do not be dismayed.
> 1 CHRONICLES 22:11-13

In Psalms 119, the chapter is covered with references to the importance of character and following God's law. Here are two verses that are really spectacular that come out of the 176 verses:

> To all perfection I see a limit, but your commands are boundless. Oh, how I love your law! I meditate on it all day long. Your commands are always with me and make me wiser than my enemies.
> PSALMS 119: 96-98 NIV

Therefore, your Character is key in following Christ. It is the odometer to your true heart stance. God cares first about your heart. Your character is the clearest gauge of your true heart stance. It's like a lie-detector test. Your character reveals where your heart stands. Here are a few additional verses on the importance of the heart:

> Realize that they come to test your faith and to produce in you the quality of endurance. But let the process go on until that endurance is fully developed, and you will find you have become men of mature character with the right sort of independence.
> JAMES 1:3–4 PHILLIPS

> Show yourself as one who owes his strength to the truth of the faith he has absorbed and the sound teaching he has followed. But steer clear of all these stupid Godless fictions. Take time and trouble to keep yourself spiritually fit. Bodily fitness has a certain value, but spiritual fitness is essential both for this present life and for the life to come.
> 1 TIMOTHY 4:6B-8 PHILLIPS

[Additional verses can be found in Deuteronomy 28:13 and throughout Psalm 119.]

Suitcase Characteristics

We know that God values humility, faith, and discipline by the scriptures in Philippians 2, Hebrews 11, and Hebrews 12, respectively. Please read these chapters to have a fuller understanding of each.

In all, the key foundations of the gospel outline God's grace in our lives on everything.

Appendix B

Framework of PBY

Purpose Built Young is a highly-structured work.

The book operates in clearly organized parts and sections so that you can constantly refer to your most relevant needs of any season. Need to brush up on your understanding of humility? See Part II, Humility, Topic: Overview. Need to regain the confidence in your ability to pioneer? Check out Part III, Chase The Fears. Everything is made for the on-the-go person looking for micro-moments to capture their journey.

Three Parts

This book is divided up into 3 major parts: Your Story, Your Character, and Your Future.

Part 1: Your Story details the current state of your life and outlines the first topic, purpose.

Part 2: Your Character details the Suitcase Characteristics (humility, faith, and discipline). Anywhere you go, these three characteristics must go with you.

Part 3: Your Future details a highly misunderstood topic: pioneering. What you do with what you got is the straightest scale to measure a pioneer.

Five Topics

PBY covers five topics—purpose, humility, faith, discipline, and pioneering—in an all-encompassing form.

Before we go any further, here is a core statement of each topic:

Purpose: Purpose is unconditional; your choice to fulfill it is optional

Humility: Understanding your place with God

Faith: Initiating your walk towards God

Discipline: Allowing you to place yourself before God

Pioneer: What you do, with what you got

Within the 3 major parts are 5 topics that detail the overview of the topic, what culture asks about the topic, and how this changes your life. Each section includes a Go! Guide that helps you take to life with this knowledge.

The 3P's

An important aspect of understanding your internal sovereignty is defining what influences it.

You can be a CEO and be completely living against your purpose. In the same way, you can be a janitor at an elementary school with purpose in every sweep, flush, and wash.

The 3P's are:

Position: Your stance in life in regard to others. As your work, family, and social constructs matter, so does your position.

Power: Your ability to leverage and influence others.

Possessions: Your things. This could be wealth, property, a car, clothing, or a social account.

References

Bible Reference:
English Standard Version
(unless otherwise noted)

Preface
[1] http://blogs.wsj.com/economics/2016/05/02/
student-debt-is-about-to-set-another-record-but-
the-picture-isnt-all-bad/

[2] Salenbacher, Jürgen. Creative Personal Brand-
ing. Netherlands: BIS Publishers, 2013.

Why Character
[1] Article in The Atlantic by Paul Tough:
http://www.theatlantic.com/magazine/ar-
chive/2016/06/how-kids-really-succeed/480744/

Introduction
[1] Encyclopedia of The Bible - Sea of Galilee:
https://www.biblegateway.com/resources/ency-
clopedia-of-the-bible/Sea-Galilee

Your Most Ambitious Goal
[1] https://www.ted.com/talks/joseph_kim_the_
family_i_lost_in_north_korea_and_the_family_i_
gained?language=en

The Call—The Power of Young People
[1] United Nations, Department of Economic and
Social Affairs, Population Division (2015). World
Population Prospects: The 2015 Revision. New
York: United Nations.

Kardia: The Heart's Desire
[1] 1 Samuel 16:7b ESV

Purpose: Overview
[1] https://www.ted.com/talks/thomas_thwaites_
how_i_built_a_toaster_from_scratch?language=en

Purpose's Challenger: Your Dark Voice
[1] https://www.ted.com/talks/barry_schwartz_on_
the_paradox_of_choice?language=en

Humility: Overview
[1] http://www.dictionary.com/browse/humble

[2] Seth Godin writes about being the best in the
world in his books Linchpin: Are You Indispensable? and The Dip: A Little Book That Teaches
You When to Quit. Jim Collins writes about being
the best in the world in his book: Good to Great:
Why Some Companies Make the Leap...and
Others Don't

Humility: Culture Asks
[1] https://www.ted.com/talks/seth_godin_on_
sliced_bread?language=en

Faith: How Does This Change Your Life?
[1] Manning, Brennan. Ruthless Trust: The Raga-
muffin's Path to God. HarperCollins, 2002.

Discipline: How Does This Change Your Life?
[1] http://fundersandfounders.com/too-late-to-
start-life-crisis/

About the Author

David Iskander is a first generation American.
His parents migrated from Egypt in the late 80s.
He grew up in Long Beach, CA and found
a personal relationship with Jesus at 21 years old.

He is a student of life. Currently, David's vision
is to bring inspiration and compassion to every pioneer*.

*If you have a spirit, you are a pioneer.

41470998R00184

Made in the USA
San Bernardino, CA
13 November 2016